Native Athletes

IN ACTION!

Vincent Schilling

NATIVE VOICES
Summertown, Tennessee

Library of Congress Cataloging-in-Publication Data

Names: Schilling, Vincent.
Title: Native athletes in action / Vincent Schilling.
Description: Revised edition. | Summertown, TN : 7th Generation, [2016]
Identifiers: LCCN 2015050158 (print) | LCCN 2016006335 (ebook) | ISBN 9781939053145 (pbk.) | ISBN 9781939053855 (E-book)
Subjects: LCSH: Indian athletes—Biography—Juvenile literature. | Indians of North America—Sports—Juvenile literature.
Classification: LCC GV697.A1 S415 2016 (print) | LCC GV697.A1 (ebook) | DDC 796.0922—dc23
LC record available at http://lccn.loc.gov/2015050158

We chose to print this title on responsibly harvested paper stock certified by The Forest Stewardship Council®, an independent auditor of responsible forestry practices. For more information, visit https://us.fsc.org.

Cover and interior design: John Wincek
Stock photography: 123 RF

Printed in the United States of America

7th Generation
a division of Book Publishing Company
PO Box 99
Summertown, TN 38483
888-260-8458
bookpubco.com

ISBN: 978-1-93905-314-5

21 20 19 18 17 16   1 2 3 4 5 6 7 8 9

DEDICATION

This book is dedicated to my father, Ray Schilling, who taught me kindness, compassion, and honesty, and to my beautiful wife, Delores, without whom I could not have accomplished this much.

CONTENTS

ACKNOWLEDGMENTS

This book has been a fantastic journey for me, as well as a great gift. I spoke with amazing athletes who were full of enthusiasm and humility. Their accomplishments have been impressive. I feel honored to have transcribed their life's efforts. (I hope I have done all of you justice.)

I would like to thank Warren Jefferson, Jerry Hutchens, Gwynelle Dismukes, and Bob Holzapfel, who led me through the publishing process with kind words, constructive criticism and friendly advice. Thank you so much. I would also like to thank Henry Martin for his moral support and use of his resources. Thank you to those who have shown their loving support: Mary Schilling, Sharon Anderson, Mary and Parker Keller. And once again, thanks to a group of incredibly talented athletes whose lives will help shape and improve the lives and aspirations of a new generation of athletes.

PHOTO CREDITS

Ross Anderson

Courtesy of Ross Anderson (rossanderson.org)

Cheri Becerra-Madsen

Courtesy of Cheri Becerra-Madsen

Kenny Dobbs

Courtesy of Kenny Dobbs (kennydobbs.com)

Shelly Hruska

Courtesy of Shelly Hruska

Beau Kemp

Courtesy of Chuck Henkel, Rochester Red Wings Media Relations

Naomi Lang

Photographs 1 and 3 courtesy of Barry Mittan (jbmittan.com)

Photographs 2, 4, and 5 courtesy of Leslie A. Dixon

Alwyn Morris

Photograph 1, 3, and 4 courtesy of Crombie McNeill, Athlete Information Bureau and Canadian Olympic Association

Photographs 2 and 5 courtesy of Alwyn Morris and his parents

Stephanie Murata

Courtesy of John Sachs (tech-fall.com)

Delby Powless

Courtesy of Rutgers Athletics, Rutgers University

Shoni Schimmel

Courtesy of Amy Morris, Cira Photography and Design (amy@ciraphotography.com)

Jim Thorpe

Courtesy of Cumberland County Historical Society, Carlisle, Pennsylvania

Jordin Tootoo

Courtesy of Nashville Predators, Tim Darling, Media Representative

Cory Witherill

Courtesy of IMS Photo Operations (indianapolismotorspeedway.com)

INTRODUCTION

The stories you are about to read illustrate how to make a dream come true and still stay connected to the family and heritage that are part of your inner strength. In every case these dreams were nurtured by family, friends, or coaches, or a combination of supporters. Delby Powless credits his coach, Paul Wehrum, with putting him on the right track at a time when partying proved to be a distraction for him. Shoni Schimmel worked hard to become a WNBA star with the support of her family, including her sister Jude. The majority of people in this book had tremendous support from their families, whether the athletes were adopted or lived with their biological parents.

Each of these stories begins with a dream, a vision, a desire. And each athlete set goals and proceeded to achieve them one by one, step by step. Despite obstacles, setbacks, and resistance, these men and women kept going in the direction of their heart's desire. Each of them chose not to be a victim—of circumstance or discrimination—but a victor in the game of life. Sports was the avenue that allowed them to succeed in that choice, but these same inner qualities can be applied to any path a person decides to follow.

For all of these athletes, a major source of their inner strength has been their Native heritage. This connection was powerfully demonstrated by Alwyn Morris when he bowed his head and raised an eagle feather on the Olympic platform as a symbol of his Native roots and the spiritual messenger that had visited him during his training.

Often there were many difficulties to overcome, proving success is the embodiment of talent and perseverance. Cory Witherill showed incredible perseverance in the face of multiple serious injuries to win his spot in the Indy 500 championship race. Though Kenny Dobbs made a series of poor choices, he was granted a miracle after praying to his Creator and decided to forever change his life for the better. And then there is Cheri Becerra-Madsen, who triumphed over a triple set of obstacles. As she explains it, "I'm not only a Native, I'm also a woman, and in a wheelchair." Cheri became an Olympic and Paralympic medal winner, as well as a world-record holder in her field.

All of these athletes have used their success to be a force for good in their own communities. Almost everyone in this book has an organization, program, or affiliation that promotes opportunities for Native youth, or they have opened the door for Native people in a sport where there had been no people of color at all. In giving back, these athletes have made their success complete, for they are nurturing a new generation with the potential to achieve even more.

Sports itself offers many benefits. The physical activity involved can help thwart obesity, diabetes, and other health-related problems that currently face Native and non-Native youth alike. The guidance, direction, and self-discipline that sports provide can help raise self-esteem and steady progress toward a chosen goal can be an ongoing source of empowerment. Time spent in athletics means less time spent in boring isolation or engaging in destructive behaviors, and local sports events create opportunities for social interaction and bonding among families and neighbors.

People of all colors, genders, ages, and occupations can be motivated and guided by these stories. I hope they will open you up to new possibilities for your life or give you added motivation to continue on your chosen path. Whatever your circumstances, I encourage you to dream an amazing dream for yourself and then go out and live it.

—Vincent Schilling

Native Athletes

IN ACTION!

CHAPTER 1

Kenny Dobbs

(CHOCTAW)

BASKETBALL DUNKING CHAMPION

Kenny Dobbs has certainly made his mark on this world—much of it from midair! At the young age of twenty-seven, Kenny began entering basketball-dunking contests and soon became widely recognized for his

Kenny Dobbs

unusual style and skill. Since then, Kenny—aka "The Dunk Inventor"—has toured the globe with the National Basketball Association (NBA) and Sprite as a celebrity dunker for sold-out shows and halftime exhibitions.

Dobbs's dunks are so creative that video-game maker 2K Sports asked his permission to replicate them in the best-selling basketball video game NBA 2K13. So when gamers maneuver one of the NBA player's avatars to the hoop for a dunk, chances are good that they're seeing copies of Kenny Dobbs's moves!

But it isn't his dunking skill that means the most to Kenny. As someone who knows what trouble is, he has dedicated himself to delivering messages of hope and strength to Native young people through the organization he founded, Uprise Youth Movement.

He is able to share this message of empowerment because his own life has been an example of overcoming difficulties to achieve great success. Things haven't always been so positive for this slam-dunk champ. As a kid, Dobbs got involved with gangs and drugs and lived a life of crime. After being arrested for robbery and evading the police at the age of seventeen, Dobbs faced the possibility of a considerable prison sentence. It took a dramatic and terrifying turn of events to set him on the path to a better life.

Born on St. Patrick's Day in 1984 in Phoenix, Arizona, Dobbs recalls a childhood filled with partying adults, illegal drugs, and encounters with a lot of questionable people. He remembers one occasion when his father screamed for his gun as he tried to stop three men from entering their home, the result of a drug deal gone wrong.

Unfortunately, such circumstances were normal for Dobbs. He started using drugs with friends when he was eleven years old. The basketball court was one of his few escapes. He idolized players such as Michael Jordan and Dominique Wilkins, but looking up to these role models wasn't enough to affect the choices he made day to day.

By age thirteen Dobbs was smoking marijuana regularly and managed to get kicked out of sixth grade. Within a few years he had already run away from home several times, had dropped out of high school, and was selling drugs.

There were some positive influences in Kenny Dobbs's life. Kenny's older cousin, known to the family as "Big Rick," had turned his own life around and saw that Kenny was heading down the wrong path. Big Rick tried to teach Kenny how to live life in a positive way. "He pressed me because he knew he was a leading force," said Kenny. "When Big Rick changed his life, I knew it was a priority and a goal for him to get me to change my life. He told me, 'You gotta get it right.'"

Shortly after changing his life for the better, Big Rick died of an illness. Soon after, Rick's mother had a dream that profoundly affected Kenny. "She told me that Big Rick said to her in her dream for me 'to get it right.' That really hit me hard, to know that he was telling me that and to hear her say that."

Although Kenny says he never forgot about his cousin's words, he was stubborn and continued to get into trouble. "That was a spark," he says. "But I didn't change my life right away. It took me another two and a half years. I'm the type of person who is very stubborn. If I get burned by the fire, I'll touch it again.

"It took me extra time to learn my lesson. It wasn't until after I was arrested for robbery and I was looking at nine years in prison and my back was up against the wall that I realized that I needed to make changes."

When he was seventeen, Kenny and his friends tried to rob a furniture store. After their botched attempt, the police followed and later caught Kenny. He was told he would be facing from six to nine years in prison.

Kenny Dobbs

Released to await trial, Dobbs went out to party while his younger sister slept in his room. During the time he was gone, gunmen drove by and shot up the front of his house. Their bullets barely missed Dobbs's sister, who was lucky to not be killed. When Dobbs returned to a home nearly destroyed by shotguns, he found that his family had already changed the locks. His mother would not let him in the house, and when he tried to enter anyway, she slapped him in the face.

"It was a moment that affected me and my family, and my eyes were opened," said Dobbs. At this very low point, he knew that he needed to change his life or he was going to die.

After years of making bad mistakes and getting into trouble, Kenny finally decided to ask for guidance. He got down on his knees and prayed to his Creator. He asked for a miracle and promised that if he received one, he would change his life forever.

Later, at his trial, both the police officer and the witness against Kenny failed to show up. This is something that Dobbs's attorney said he had never seen happen before. Dobbs was fined $5,000 for evading the police but was spared any further incarceration.

"When the judge read off my sentence and told me I wouldn't serve any time, my attorney looked me and said, 'It is a miracle you're not going to prison.'"

Kenny had received his miracle. Now he had a promise to keep.

That day, Dobbs was given a second chance at life. He made a decision to succeed and to turn his life around, and he started making positive life choices.

Having only earned three high school credits before dropping out, Dobbs enrolled in an accelerated learning program and went back to school. For eighteen months, he worked from 7:30 a.m. to 6:30 p.m. at his studies, and he graduated with a high school diploma in 2003. He also paid his parents back for the $5,000 fine they had covered for him. In 2005 he married his girlfriend and they had a baby girl; her name, Uriya, means "Light of God."

Kenny went to work for the Division of Behavioral Health Services in Arizona and served as chairman on the Arizona State Youth Advisory Council for alcohol and substance abuse prevention. He later enrolled at Glendale Community College and began to play basketball, immediately impressing his teammates and coaches with his jumping and dunking prowess.

Through good and bad, basketball has remained a true passion for Kenny. "I really started playing basketball when I was probably about ten years old, when I got my first hoop. It was one of those adjustable hoops; my dad put it up to ten feet, and he never wanted me to lower it. When I got home from school, after my dad had gone to work, I would put it down to about seven or eight feet and have dunk-offs.

"I realized I had this talent for dunking after my first dunk in the summer of eighth grade. It was just a regular dunk, but ever since that happened, it was nonstop every day after school. We would play our games, and once one game was done, we would all test it out. Some of my friends were getting higher than me, so it motivated me to keep jumpin'."

In 2008 Kenny entered his first Hoop It Up dunk contest. His performance made it to YouTube, and as a result Kenny was invited to the 2008 Shaquille O'Neal Dunkman contest in Los Angeles. He later competed at the NBA All-Star Weekend and the Ball Up's Air Up There Slam Dunk Contest judged by 1992 NBA Slam Dunk champion Cedric Ceballos and NBA pro Julius Erving.

After winning several competitions, Kenny was asked to join the Sprite Slam Dunk Showdown tour and performed in several events covered by Fox Sports and ESPN.

HOW HIGH DOES KENNY JUMP?

With a vertical leap of 48 inches—that's four feet (1.2 m)!—Kenny Dobbs measures up to such basketball dunking greats as Darrell Griffith, aka "Dr. Dunkenstein," of the Utah Jazz, and Michael Jordan of the Chicago Bulls. Both of these famous players achieved 48-inch jumps during their basketball careers, and no other NBA stars have leaped higher. One of the tricks Dobbs performs at dunking expos is jumping over the heads of one or more kids to reach the goal. With four feet between him and the ground, he can clear a seven-year-old of average height.

Kenny started getting calls from other organizations too, including one group called Flying 101, a dunk team that gave exhibitions all over the world. Kenny signed up and toured with Flying 101, displaying his slam-dunk style to international audiences.

He continued to improve his jumping skills and hoped that the possibility of playing for the NBA might become a reality if he continued to work hard. He trained with James Cooper, who had worked for the Los Angeles Lakers, and he studied the physiology of slam dunking and basketball. He increased his jump from 45 to 48 inches (114 to 121 cm), a height reached by only a handful of the world's most successful basketball players.

"I started doing research, watching endless hours of dunk contests online," says Kenny. "I studied my competitors. I wanted to find out what punches they threw and have a counterpunch."

Kenny Dobbs

In 2008 Kenny created the Uprise Youth Movement. For Uprise, he travels around the country giving exhibitions of his slam-dunk skills and speaking to kids and teens at school assemblies and special events. Kenny shares stories from his own tough childhood and encourages young people to make wise choices, overcome obstacles, and achieve their goals. He also serves as an ambassador of the Native American Basketball Invitational Foundation, another organization dedicated to encouraging and empowering young people to improve their lives.

Despite all that he has accomplished, Kenny keeps aiming higher. On February 23, 2012, he competed in the Sprite Slam Dunk Showdown, judged by dunking legends Darryl Dawkins and LeBron James, during the NBA All-Star Weekend. After wowing the crowd with his unique and spectacular dunks, Kenny wiped out his competition by bringing out three people to jump over and performing a between-the-legs, over-their-heads slam dunk—while blindfolded! Accepting the trophy from LeBron James, Kenny kissed it and looked out to the crowd in triumph. He'd been nicknamed the Dunk Inventor early on, but now he was being acknowledged as the "Best Dunker in the World"!

Kenny's continued success brought him a lot of attention, and he received a call from the NBA's Dallas Mavericks. After training hard he was drafted to the Mavericks' Development League (D-League) team, the Texas Legends. Kenny had to make a tough decision: should he give up his major sponsorships as a slam-dunk champion to live his dream and play for the NBA? He had to try.

As a D-League team member, Kenny made a small fraction of his previous income, but he continued to work hard and do his best. Fate intervened, however, when a player fell on Kenny's leg, fracturing his foot and damaging his knee. He made no income as an injured reserve player.

"I was out there chasing my goal and my dream in the NBA, and I was allowed the opportunity to get it out of my system. I had doubted if I was even good enough to play."

But he had indeed played for the NBA, and while healing from his injury, Kenny realized he had been on the right path before he joined the Legends. Even though several teams wanted him, he decided to return to his first passions: slam dunking and reaching out to help young people.

Once he healed, Kenny began touring again. He created a slam-dunk mobile app that people can use to upload videos of their best slam dunks for votes and prizes. He even has his own comic book and instructional DVD.

On his tours, Dobbs is especially drawn to rural and Native communities that might not ever be able to see a live NBA game. Kenny explains his reasoning this way: "I want to deliver a positive message of hope. I want to create a movement for young people to become leaders.

"I feel so good that finally, for the first time, I know where I want to go and where I want to be. I know exactly what I want to do; I know what I'm called to do. I'm doing speaking and I'm doing dunking. I have options to go in any direction, but I know I want to reach as many youth with my message as possible."

Kenny has a message for anyone who wants to have a better and more successful life. "The power is believing in yourself and believing that you can achieve anything. That's what made the difference for me. I began believing that I could graduate from high school. I began believing that I could become a world champion. I began believing that I could make it to the NBA. By believing in that, I began to structure my time.

"No longer was I partying or wasting my time drinking or using drugs. If it did not lead me toward my goal, then it was holding me back, and I began to cut those things out.

"All of the friends that you are choosing to hang out with—are they building you up? Are they encouraging you and pushing you toward your dreams? Or are they holding you back? Are they pulling you further and further away from the path that will lead you to devoting your time to train, practice, or study?

"I wanted to increase my vertical leap, so I began studying. Instead of wasting my time playing video games, I was looking up jump workout programs on the computer and spending my time and energy in those areas that were going to benefit me.

"When I handed my parents that high school diploma, it was the greatest feeling I had ever had, and I wanted to continue to have an impact on people's lives.

"One key to success for me—and I want to make sure people understand this—it wasn't until I stopped trying to do things on my own and I started to trust in God that my situation turned around. The truth is we have to rely on and believe in our Creator."

Another lesson that Kenny has learned and applies to his own life is the importance of imagining exactly where and what he wants to be. "Our minds are very powerful. So if you think you can become what you want to be—or if you think you can't—you are right."

CHAPTER 2

Shoni Shimmel

(UMATILLA)

PROFESSIONAL WOMEN'S BASKETBALL PLAYER

In April 2014, Shoni Schimmel, a member of the Confederated Tribes of the Umatilla Indian Reservation in eastern Oregon, waited nervously in the lobby of the Mohegan Sun Hotel in Uncasville, Connecticut. Shoni, who was wearing a necklace from her great-grandmother, was waiting to hear the results of the WNBA draft. Becoming a professional basketball player had been her life-long dream.

Shoni Shimmel

Schimmel, a five-foot-nine (1.75 m) guard from the University of Louisville, was ranked fifth in NCAA Division I history with 387 three-point shots (just five shy of the 392 record), and she was also the first Louisville player ever to finish her college career with 2,174 points and six hundred assists. She didn't have to wait long to hear her name called; Shoni was selected eighth overall by the Atlanta Dream, making her the highest-drafted Native American player in WNBA history.

Soon after the WNBA draft, Shoni told reporters, "I was very happy to hear my name called, and the fact that it's down the road in Atlanta will make the transition even easier . . . I'm just so excited." Following her interview, she tweeted to her fans that this was "only the beginning."

In the world of women's basketball, Shoni Schimmel has earned the nicknames "The Umatilla Thrilla" and "Showtime." To people in Indian Country, she is an absolute hero.

Shoni didn't stop making an impression on the basketball court after she was drafted by the Dream. During her first rookie season in the WNBA, the twenty-two-year-old succeeded in breaking her records from high school and college. For example, in January 2014, despite being benched for the final nine minutes of a game against Memphis, Shoni beat her own previously set school record by hitting nine out of twelve three-pointers to score a game high of twenty-nine points and win the game.

At the end of her first year, Shoni was among the players chosen for the WNBA's end-of-season All-Star Game, which took place on August 1 at the Skiatook Multipurpose Activity Center in Skiatook, Oklahoma. After an impressive display of talent, Shoni became the first Native American woman—and rookie!—to win the coveted Most Valuable Player award for a WNBA All-Star Game.

On the day after the game, Shoni played basketball with one hundred Osage children. Later, addressing an excited crowd of kids and adults, she said, "We grew up on the reservation. I am always proud of being Native American because it's cool, it's awesome, and who wouldn't want to be Native American, right?"

Shoni Shimmel

Her dream-come-true career as a WNBA player didn't just happen; she had been preparing for it for years. At the age of four, Shoni began her journey into the world of basketball, playing on the grassy dirt courts of the Umatilla Indian Reservation. She would eventually have seven siblings, including her younger sister Jude, who shared her love of the game. In addition to her immediate family, Shoni had a wealth of extended family members who also lived on the rez.

Unfortunately some of Shoni's family on the reservation fell into alcoholism and drug addiction. Her mother, Ceci Moses, who had been a talented basketball player in school herself, wanted a better life for her children and accepted a position at a high school off of the reservation in Franklin, Oregon.

The decision was a tough one for Ceci, who worried that some family members might think that she considered herself better than them. In reality, she just wanted to seize this positive opportunity for her family.

Ceci began coaching the Franklin High School girls' basketball team, and Shoni joined its ranks. According to Shoni's father, Rick Schimmel, the team's standing record was four wins to twenty losses. When Shoni began playing for the team, the win-to-loss ratio flipped to twenty wins and only three losses.

In 2009, Shoni, then a junior, helped bring her last-place team into the quarterfinals. By the time she was a senior, she was receiving inquiries from colleges all over the country.

Although many colleges wanted Shoni, she eventually decided to play for the Louisville Cardinals. Her sister Jude joined her there the following year. Because Shoni and Jude had played together for so many years on and off the rez, the chemistry between them was magic. During their climb up the ladder to the NCAA Championships, social media in Indian Country exploded with words of support for the two sisters, under the hashtags #SchimmelShow and #SchimmelFinalFour.

Ultimately the Schimmel sisters did play together in the NCAA Division 1 Women's Basketball Championship (Final Four) game in 2013. Though their team lost to the University of Connecticut, Shoni and Jude had made great strides as Native American women in college basketball. ESPN announcers talked about them as the "two Indian sisters from the reservation." At about the same time, the Discovery Fit & Health channel aired *Off the Rez*, a basketball documentary about their lives playing basketball and their climb to success.

Shoni was surprised and excited to hear ESPN talking about Jude and her. "ESPN was covering the University of Louisville, but they were also talking about two little Indian girls. It was awesome because it was ESPN—you never hear that," said Shoni. "It still hadn't sunk in because this is something that doesn't ever really happen. Other than [baseball star] Jacoby Elsberry or [professional basketball player] Tahnee Robinson, how many Indians are out there doing this?"

Shoni Shimmel

Both Shoni and Jude appreciated what they had accomplished this far and hoped for equally successful professional careers. Though they worked hard, in part for a sense of personal accomplishment, they also remembered that many in Indian Country were looking up to them.

"That's the one thing our mom always put into our brains growing up," says Shoni. "You are not doing it for yourself; you are doing it for the other little Native American girls who are going to come along. They will have an example in front of them, and they will have the opportunity to go out there and do this and believe in themselves."

Her sister Jude adds, "We want to be that light of hope for younger generations. We want them to know it is possible. It's not every day you see Native Americans doing this type of thing. If you put your mind and heart into it, you can achieve anything you want."

Shoni understands that for many kids on the rez their circumstances may seem difficult or impossible to overcome. Making the leap from playing basketball on a playground or at school as a "rez baller" to playing at the college level takes strength, determination, and confidence.

Shoni Shimmel

"I just have confidence in myself to go out there and do it. I mean, no one has done it, so why not go out there and be the first one to do it? I like to be told I can't do stuff because then I want to go out there and prove I can. Why can't I go away from home, be far away, and be successful? My mom has always said, 'It is four years of your life; why not go out there and see the world?' Playing basketball, I've been able to see a lot of places and meet a lot of people. If I hadn't gone to the University of Louisville, if I had stayed back on the West Coast, I wouldn't have had the opportunity to do half of that."

Shoni Shimmel

At the end of her rookie WNBA season, Schimmel was in the fourth spot with a one-handed layup over Brittney Griner in the all-star game. She was also honored with Assist of the Year and Photo of the Year awards from her team, the Atlanta Dream. And, on December 25, 2014, ESPN's *SportsCenter* announced its top fifty plays of 2014, and Shoni earned the fortieth spot.

Sounds like an amazing year, right? Lots of people must have thought so, because the "Shoni Schimmel #23" basketball jersey was the biggest-selling jersey in the entire WNBA in 2014!

With such an incredible career and a long list of accomplishments, Shoni maintains that anyone who wants to succeed can—if they only believe.

"I would definitely say to believe in yourself. Have faith in yourself to be able to go out there, to have the courage to get off the reservation, to go to college, and to believe that you can do it. You were put on this earth for a reason. You decide what you want to do with your life. Continue with your dreams because that's what I've been doing since . . . I don't even know. I just wanted to play basketball. I've kept that dream."

And thanks to her unshakable faith and hard work, Shoni Schimmel isn't just dreaming anymore. She's living the dream—the Atlanta Dream.

ABOUT THE UMATILLA

The Umatilla tribal headquarters are located in Mission, Oregon. For the past ten years, the tribe's major focus has been restoring fish in the Umatilla and Grande Ronde Rivers. In early 1980, under the tribe's leadership, salmon were reintroduced in the Umatilla River. Today, along with the state of Oregon, the tribe operates facilities for salmon egg retrieval and spawning that are helping to restore salmon runs in these rivers. Seventy years after being driven to extinction in the Umatilla River, Chinook salmon have returned, due to the efforts and dedication of the Umatilla.

CHAPTER 3

Cheri Becerra-Madsen

(OMAHA)

WHEELCHAIR-RACING OLYMPIAN AND WORLD RECORD HOLDER

When you hear of someone with a disability, you may think of a person whose ability to perform everyday tasks is limited. But for Cheri Becerra-Madsen, a Native American of the Omaha Tribe who has been a paraplegic since the age of four, the sky's the only limit she respects. Cheri is a spectacular success: a two-time Olympian, Paralympian, and world record holder in three-wheeled wheelchair racing. She has earned respect for women, her Native heritage, and people with disabilities worldwide.

Cheri Becerra was born in Nebraska City, Nebraska. When she was four years old, a virus left her paralyzed from the waist down. "All my brothers and sisters would be out riding their bikes," she remembers. "I'd go riding too, but I couldn't keep up in my wheelchair. They were too fast." The solution? Cheri rode on the backs of their bikes. Sometimes they would tease Cheri in a goodnatured way, because she was always losing her shoes. According to Cheri, "That is so funny, because I still lose my shoes."

Cheri Becerra-Madsen

When Cheri was eighteen, a teacher friend read a magazine article about three-wheeled wheelchair racing and asked Cheri if she would be interested in going to a meet in a couple of weeks. "That was the first time I had even seen a racing chair. When I arrived, there were all these kids in these chairs, and they were really fast. I tried to compete with them in my everyday, regular chair and they smoked me!"

At the event Cheri met Jim Martinson, an amputee and Vietnam War veteran. Jim is the designer of the Shadow three-wheeled racing chair. He let Cheri use his chair in the competition, even though it wasn't a very good fit. "He was a grown man, and I was a really skinny girl. I've always been less than a hundred pounds. He was rolling up shirts and stuffing them into the chair so I wouldn't move around so much. Also, it was different from my regular chair because you race leaning over. My chest was on my lap, and I remember my back hurting because I don't think I had ever been in that position." In spite of Cheri's back pain, she found success. "I ended up beating almost everyone there—my first time ever in the chair!"

After that first race day, she considered taking up racing but did not have the $3,000 for a new three-wheeled wheelchair. Cheri was in for a big surprise. Her hometown threw a benefit that raised enough money to buy one. After that there was no stopping her.

Soon Cheri was invited to the nationals. With only two weeks to train for them, she had to learn a new way of moving in a wheelchair. "I would wear what are called harness gloves. You kind of punch the rim, so the gloves have to be able to stick to the wheel. You never grab it, just punch off on it. Your hands are always in a fist. When I went to the nationals, it was a real awakening because everybody there was fast. I thought it was going to be pretty easy. I didn't realize the competition that was out there."

Even against the best racers in the country, Cheri came in first in her age category. In fact she finished in the top three overall, losing by only a half chair length! Jim Martinson was delighted and offered to sponsor her on the spot. "He custom-fitted me with a new wheelchair. It was specialized with tri-spoke wheels and all that jazz."

At that meet Cheri made friends with wheelchair racer LeAnn Shannon. They hit it off instantly, and when LeAnn asked if Cheri would like to come to Florida to train, Cheri accepted.

Cheri proudly displays her racing equipment, Olympic jacket, and medals.

LeAnn lived in Jacksonville, Florida, and though Cheri was happy to have a new friend, she was unaccustomed to such a quiet house. “There are six kids in my family. My house was always loud—total screaming, total chaos, everybody arguing. LeAnn’s was different, but it was nice.”

Cheri and LeAnn would go to the gym early in the morning. Sometimes they would get on a hand cycle, an elongated three-wheeler peddled by the arms rather than the legs. At night they would go to the track. Cheri and LeAnn both had their sights set on the national trials, the qualifiers for the Olympic and Paralympic Games.

The Olympics offer two events for wheelchair athletes: the 1500-meter race for men and the 800-meter race for women. The Paralympics take place just after the Olympics at the Olympic sites. There are Paralympic competitions for athletes with a wide range of physical and intellectual disabilities. Through hard work and determination, Cheri eventually won enough events to qualify for the Paralympics—and after that the 1996 Olympics.

"Our regional meet would be in the United States. Then we would do our semifinal in Europe. So you have a chance of getting beat out twice before you get to the Olympics." If she did well enough in the US trials, she would get to go to the semifinals.

Well enough? She won the US trials! And it was on to Paris!

Cheri attended the Fédération Française Handisport, the training center for athletes with disabilities in France, under the guidance of US coach and wheelchair athlete

PARALYMPICS

The Paralympics were created for athletes with physical, intellectual, and sensory challenges. Competitive wheelchair racing is just one of many Paralympic events and involves the use of a specialized three-wheel racing wheelchair. Athletes can win a bronze, silver, or gold medal in the 100-, 200-, 400-, and 800-meter events.

Marty Morse. There Cheri encountered a whole new experience: discrimination.

"I'm not only a Native, I'm also a woman, and in a wheelchair. I got all these things thrown at me that I didn't even know existed until I got out there and tried to rule the world, no longer pampered by my family.

"It just hits you. A few times people in the crowd would be doing the 'hi yi yi yuh, hi yi yi yuh' thing. I was called a Yankee. I was like, 'Dude, do you know what a Yankee is? I'm a Native American. I'm so not Yankee.' But I always got the

Cheri Becerra-Madsen

war cry thing. It was dumb, but they thought it was funny." Even so, Cheri proved she was ready to handle anything. At a competition just before the Olympic trials, she broke the world record in the 400 meter!

At the Olympic trials, Cheri came in with a strong finish and found herself on the US Olympic team, along with Jean Driscoll and her friend LeAnn Shannon.

At 10:00 a.m. on August 1, 1996, Cheri was at the starting line for the 800-meter race at the Olympic Games in Atlanta, Georgia. After an intensely competitive race, she took the bronze medal with a time of 1:55.49 and became the first Native American female to win a medal in the Olympic Games.

In the Paralympics, held a couple of weeks after the closing ceremony of the Olympics, Cheri won bronze medals in the 400-meter and 800-meter races, and she took the silver in the 100-meter and 200-meter races.

At first glance Cheri Becerra had a lot to overcome, being a Native American, a woman, and a paraplegic. But nothing was going to keep her back. Right after the 1996 Paralympic Games, she began training for the Paralympic and Olympic Games that would take place in 2000 in Sydney, Australia. There she suffered a huge disappointment: she came in fifth in the women's 800-meter Olympic race.

Rather than getting depressed or angry with herself, Cheri transformed her dissatisfaction into determination. In the Sydney Paralympics, she not only won the gold medal in both the 100-meter and 400-meter races, she broke two world records!

After she retired from competition, Cheri moved to Union, a small town near Nebraska City—just a post office and a few hundred people, and most of them know each other. She is married, has two daughters, and lives next door to her mother. She believes strongly in pursuing one's dreams and speaks out against drug and alcohol abuse and other things that shatter those dreams time after time.

"If you have a dream, you've got to focus on it and do it. It's really important to be involved in sports or some extracurricular activity that is going to be a positive influence. I can't wait for my girls to grow up and be involved in sports. It's going to be so cool."

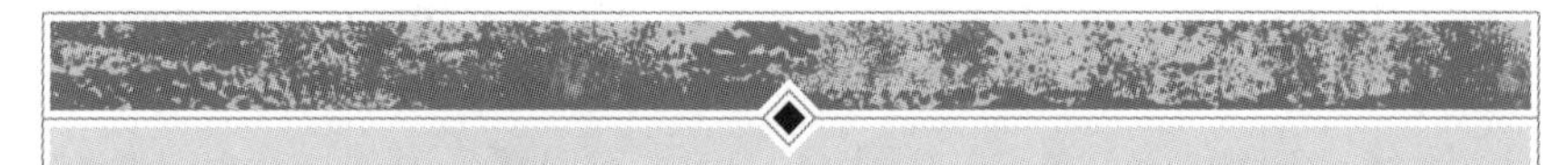

ABOUT THE OMAHA

Over six thousand Omaha live near their ancestors' original settlements along the Missouri River in eastern Nebraska and a small portion of Iowa. Their traditional base, now part of the Omaha Indian Reservation and adjacent counties, totals 2,594 square miles. A treaty with the United States signed on March 16, 1854, established the Omaha Tribe's legal hold on reservation lands.

CHAPTER 4

Cory Witherill

(NAVAJO)

INDY RACE CAR DRIVER

Few people will ever know the thrill of hurtling around a racetrack at 230 miles per hour (370 kph). Cory Witherill does. In 2001 he became the first Native American driver to race in the Indianapolis 500.

Cory Witherill's mother was from the Navajo Nation, near the Four Corners region where Arizona, Utah, Colorado, and New Mexico meet. She was only eighteen when she became pregnant and felt that she could barely take care of herself, let alone an infant. Wanting the best for her baby, she put him up for adoption.

Cory Witherill

Cory became the youngest of Liston and Carol Witherill's ten official children. The Witherills had an amazing way with kids, and their unofficial family was much larger than ten.

Youngsters who had no place to go or who had a difficult family life were always welcomed and given support and guidance. The Witherills stressed self-esteem and hard work. Cory remembers one boy in particular. “My brother met him down at the beach. My mom fed him and gave him a place to live on one condition: ‘Turn your life around and be something,’ she said. He did. Today he’s a fireman—my dad got him into the fire academy.”

The family spent summer vacations at Lake Arrowhead, California, and it was there that Cory got his first taste of speed. Every year his family rented all-terrain vehicles (ATVs), and by the age of twelve he was racing around on his own. When a family friend decided to sell a Suzuki 185, it became Cory’s Christmas present. By the end of Christmas Day, he and his brothers had carved out a mini racetrack in the front yard.

Cory was fourteen when he competed in his first ATV race at Ascot Park in Gardena, California. Despite being very nervous, he came in third. Cory went into his second race hungry for first place. “I caught up to the guy who was running second, and I passed him. I was getting a good momentum when I landed off a jump on a weird angle.” He zoomed off the track and crashed into a parked van.

Despite torn ligaments and a broken ankle, Cory plunged back into racing. His parents agreed to support him, provided he stay away from drugs, stay in school, and get good grades. If his grades fell, he couldn’t race.

While in high school, Cory broke his wrist during a race, but that didn’t stop him. He was still wearing the splint in one of his last amateur ATV contests. “I think I was in fourth place. The sun was going down, and the track was really dusty. The four of us were bumper to bumper, and I caught the glare of the sun and dust. The guy in front of me slammed on his brakes and we collided. Next thing I knew, we were both flying over our handlebars. His ATV landed on my arm and fractured the two forearm bones.”

The result? Two plates and fourteen surgical screws remain in his arm.

Cory's doctors told him to quit racing. They said if he fell the wrong way, the metal could shatter the bones in his arm beyond repair. Cory still wanted the speed and adrenaline rush of competing, so he compromised. He decided to race dune buggies since they came with seat belts!

Over the next few years, his wins included five Motocross Valvoline de Montréal Championships and two PACE US Stadium Off Road Championships. To this day he is "the man to beat" in off-road racing.

In 2000 Cory passed the Indy Racing League rookie test. That made him eligible to compete in the Indy Lights, a series of races that allow drivers to develop their skills in Formula 2000 cars, which are lighter versions of IndyCars that also go slower—about 140 miles per hour (225 kph).

During one of the races, Cory was driving at 130 mph (209 kph). "The Formula 2000 cars are safe," he says, "but

INDY AUTO RACING

The Indianapolis 500 is the fastest long-distance car race of its kind in the world. Held annually on Memorial Day, this race is known for cars that travel at an average of 200 miles per hour (321.8 kph). Race car drivers must possess the ability to drive for extended periods of time. They must also have endurance and quick reflexes and use their intuition in order to handle such high-powered race cars. Although all of these skills are important, proper care and maintenance of the vehicle by a pit crew can make the difference between winning and losing a race.

they're mainly for road-course racing. They have an all-metal tubular frame, which is not designed to take a hard impact, and going into turn three, I got hit. I compressed and fractured my T6 vertebra. I had to have a back brace on for about eight weeks." Cory was taken off the course in an ambulance but was back racing a mere twelve weeks later.

As the cars he drove got faster, racing became more physical, so Cory decided to step up his physical training. He made a bet with a friend that he'd stick to it—and he did, jogging every morning and going to the gym. Within three months, Cory went from 183 to 167 pounds (83 to 76 kg), greatly improved his fitness level, and found it easier to control his vehicle.

In 2001 Cory was asked to race for a team that had competitors in the Indianapolis 500. To qualify, he had to have one of the thirty-three fastest runs. Sound easy? Maybe not. The time between first and last place is less than one second.

Cory had three days to get his speed over 220 mph (354 kph), but for the first two days he could not do it. He had never driven at such speeds.

"When I was coming out of turn four I could see an airplane in the corner of my eye. A plane lands at 200 miles (322 km) an hour and I was passing the airplane when it was coming down for a landing. That was my eye opener. But I was only going 219 [352 kph], and running out of time."

His team decided to change the degree of placement of his tires by a mere four millimeters, but after four practice laps, Cory asked them to adjust it to two millimeters. He had one hour left in which to qualify! All of his training and years of dedication came down to his speed in the last four laps.

He was one of the last drivers to secure a spot at 221 mph (355.6 kph). "I qualified on the final hour of bump day, the third day," Cory says. He went on to become the first full-blood Native American to qualify for the Indy 500.

Cory's success depends a lot on working closely with his pit crew.

There were four hundred thousand people at Indianapolis Motor Speedway during the Memorial Day weekend in late May 2001. Cory recalls that the bleachers were as high and wide as in a football stadium on both sides, pretty much all the way down the front straightaway to the first turn. "It was wall-to-wall people!" The drivers arrived at six in the morning and still needed police escorts to ease them through the throngs of race fans.

Cory started in thirty-first place but soon made his way up to twelfth, competing against drivers he had admired for years—Al Unser Jr., Johnny Rutherford, Michael Andretti, Jimmy Vasser, and Rick Mears. In lap 140, he caught up to Arie Luyendyk, two-time winner of the Indy 500. "I had him locked in my sights. I was gaining on him, and I would've probably been able to pass him."

Suddenly Cory's car spun out of control. He'd run over some debris and punctured a tire, which sent his car heading for the wall. "I just closed my eyes and braced myself and waited for the impact. Two cars were coming straight at me. It looked like they were going to T-bone me. But then they locked up the brakes and turned away. Meanwhile, I was sliding sideways down the front straightaway. I missed the wall by about a foot."

Cory's car was towed back to the pit; the team worked feverishly and got him back in the race. By now he was down ten laps and in twenty-sixth place, but he worked his way up to nineteenth before time ran out.

"When I came back from Indy, my brother gave me a big hug. I showed him a picture taken a half hour before the race—they have all the drivers line up at the start/finish line. Then it all sunk in! This was something I had wanted to do when I was a kid, something I spent my whole life working on. I was like, Wow—did I just do that?"

With hard work and dedication, Cory lived one dream, but he has many more. He hopes to become the first Native American to win both the Indy 500 and the Daytona 500. He also dreams of becoming the first Native American to race full time for a NASCAR team.

Cory's biggest dream, however, is to stop the rise of diabetes among Native Americans. In 2003 he created a program called Team Diabetes Racing (TDR) to encourage Native Americans to take control of their health. He travels around the country making presentations to raise awareness about diabetes and the importance of exercise and proper diet.

Cory also encourages young people to stay away from smoking, drugs, and alcohol, and to follow their dreams. He has even established an internship program to help Native American kids interested in racing achieve their goals. To the young people he talks with, he says, "You really have to want to do it. Otherwise, you're just wasting your time. Like anything in life, if you do it, you have to do it right."

ABOUT THE NAVAJO

The Navajo Nation covers twenty-five thousand square miles, situated within the exterior boundaries of Arizona, New Mexico, and Utah. There are approximately 225,000 members of the Navajo Nation, making it the largest federally recognized Indian tribe in the United States. Several thousand nonmembers also reside and work there.

CHAPTER 5

Alwyn Morris

(MOHAWK)

OLYMPIC GOLD MEDALIST IN KAYAKING

Standing on the Olympic podium to receive a gold medal is probably the peak of any athlete's career. When kayaker Alwyn Morris stood there at the 1984 Summer Olympics medal ceremonies, he proudly held aloft an eagle feather to honor those who had helped him achieve his dream—his family, his Mohawk ancestors, and Canada. Alwyn and his kayaking partner, Hugh Fisher, won both bronze and gold medals for their efforts that year.

Alwyn Morris was born in 1957 in the Mohawk territory of Kahnawake, south of Montreal, Quebec. The Kahnawake kids didn't have any league sports, but they played hockey in the winter and lacrosse and a little bit of baseball in the summer. Alwyn also spent his free time with friends swimming in the nearby lake.

Alwyn grew up in a disciplined atmosphere. Both his strict Catholic family and highly regimented Catholic school handed out harsh penalties for misbehavior. Alwyn had to go to confession daily and to Mass three or four times a week. If he wanted spending money, he had to earn it, which he did by caddying at the local golf course.

Alwyn was especially close to his grandfather, Tom Morris. Tom became very sick while Alwyn was still quite young, so Alwyn moved in with his grandparents to help his grandmother. After Tom recovered, Alwyn stayed on at their place and learned valuable lessons from them.

"When you have grandparents around you, you learn to appreciate the quality of the individual, because they're coming from a point of wisdom and experience that is far deeper than anyone else's."

Alwyn's grandfather had been a successful athlete, prominent in both lacrosse and hockey, and was a wonderful role model for his young grandson.

In 1968, while watching the Mexico City Summer Olympics on TV, Alwyn announced that he was going to be in the Olympics someday. When Tom asked his grandson if he realized how much work that would involve, twelve-year-old Alwyn told him that no amount of work was too much. He was determined to be an Olympian even though he hadn't chosen a sport.

Fate stepped in when the Onake Paddling Club opened up in Kahnawake the year Alwyn turned fifteen. He joined and before long was on the first rung of the ladder to his Olympic dream. But Alwyn was small and thin. His coaches didn't think he would ever amount to any kind of real athlete. Was he going to let that stop him? "Is being small a hurdle? If you let that take control of you, it will be! There are a lot of things that make up an athlete. It's not just about size; it's not just about strength. It's a combina-

Alwyn Morris

Alwyn and his grandfather, Tom Morris, in 1958.

tion of many different pieces that give you the fortitude and other characteristics to compete at the highest level."

No matter what people said—bystanders, teammates, or even coaches—Alwyn was going to prove them wrong with discipline, drive, and positive thinking. Soon his hard work began to pay off. His club coach, Kenneth Deer, noticed that instead of just hanging out with friends or getting into trouble, Alwyn was always on the water practicing. In time he became the club's number-one paddler. He progressed steadily and started to win some competitions.

The motivation behind all this practice and dedication was advice he had received from his grandfather. "If you intend to get anywhere," Tom Morris had told him, "you not only have to work hard, but you also have to ask yourself a couple of questions. First, did you give all that you possibly could? If you answer yes, then you have to be satisfied and move on. If you answer no, you have to ask, why didn't I? Second, did I get as much out of this day as I possibly could have or did I cheat myself?"

In 1975, two special things happened: Alwyn won the Canadian national junior championships, and tryouts for the 1976 Olympics were held in Montreal. Because of his national win, Alwyn and his doubles partner, Jean Fournel, were invited to compete for a place on the Canadian Olympic team. The pair made it to the finals, although they did not place.

Alwyn said, “I missed it by a bit, but trying to make the Olympic team in 1976 had its major benefits the following year, because I was able to get to a much higher level of training.”

It was the possibility of advanced training that forced Alwyn to make one of the biggest decisions of his life. The best training in Canada was in Burnaby, British Columbia, almost three thousand miles west. Three thousand miles from parents, friends, and most importantly, from his grandfather. Although it would be lonely being separated from the people who were important to him, Alwyn decided to go to Burnaby.

There the young paddler met and became friends with Hugh Fisher, who would eventually become his Olympic partner. He also received a gift that was both an inspiration and a wonder: “A great bald eagle would come to the training site every spring and every fall and sit on these big, big trees or perch on top of the poles that marked out our kayaking course.”

The eagle has the keenest sight of all birds and flies the highest. It is said to be the earth creature closest to the world of the Spirit, and a messenger who carries people’s hopes and prayers to the Creator.

KAYAKING

A kayak is similar to a canoe except the pilot is enclosed within a kayak and a canoe is open to the elements. The paddle of a kayak has a blade at both ends, and the operator can paddle with both arms alternately with a smooth, fluid motion. Kayaking is one of the oldest forms of transportation in the world, having been developed by the Aleuts of the Arctic regions of America and Greenland.

Alwyn and Hugh's faces show the determination and perseverance that are required to succeed in sports or any endeavor.

"So I started to speak to him in my Mohawk language; it just seemed to be the right thing to do. And when I spoke Mohawk, the eagle perked up. He moved his head as if he understood, while I drifted in my kayak next to his post.

"I continued to speak to him, and all the other guys were like, 'Look, he's listening to you!' It was so cool. This majestic bird just stood there and listened to the words I was saying and allowed us to approach so close. It was only after I paddled away that he took off. Knowing the range of these birds and that each one controls certain areas, my assumption is that it was the same bird that came every year."

Alwyn had his sights set on the 1980 Moscow Olympics, but he knew he would be up against superb competition. He knew that he would have to be prepared both mentally and physically in order to do well.

"I feel there are two main approaches to facing a competitor. The first approach is to go after your competitor as if you're saying, 'I hate you so much I want to beat you.' The other approach is to say, 'I respect how good you are and that respect will help me to beat you.' I saw my competitors as athletes who had skill, who had potential, who trained really hard. That has to be recognized and respected. Not everybody goes for that. Some people go for the throat; but it has never worked for me."

Alwyn made the Canadian Olympic team in singles, but then all of the country's Olympic athletes were dealt a devastating blow. Canada joined sixty-four other nations in an Olympic boycott. They would not send teams to compete in the games in Moscow because the USSR had invaded Afghanistan. This was a terrible letdown for Alwyn. "I was ranked in the top three kayakers in the world for the 1000-meter singles race. It was a huge disappointment."

Alwyn holds up the eagle feather as he and Hugh Fisher accept the Olympic medal.

It was all the more disappointing because at about this time Alwyn's grandfather died. Tom Morris would never see his grandson in Olympic competition.

"I could've gotten stuck then—given up on it all—but the goal was still there. That's when Hugh Fisher and I partnered up, and from there we just took it forward." Forward all the way to the 1984 Olympics in Los Angeles, California.

Alwyn and Hugh were favorites in the 500-meter and 1000-meter kayak doubles. After a bad start in the 500-meter race, they pressed hard enough to win the bronze. They were disappointed but tried to shake it off, laughing and joking to help them refocus.

In the 1000-meter race, the German team got off to a really great start; Alwyn and Hugh were trailing. Alwyn knew that the Germans planned to go hard all the way, but there was no way they would be able to keep up their initial pace. The Canadian team had a chance! As the Germans tired, Alwyn and Hugh took the lead and never gave it back.

It was a moving moment when Alwyn stood on the podium to receive his gold medal, holding up that eagle feather. It was widely publicized and brought attention to the culture of indigenous people. Alwyn—the Canadian-Mohawk Olympic hero, the skinny kid who would never become an athlete—came home to a hero's welcome, cheered on by thousands of proud well-wishers.

His Olympic gold medal brought new opportunities and honors. The National Native Role Model Program sent him into the Native communities to encourage youth to develop their potential and pursue their dreams.

"I always hope that somewhere someone is going to get the message I got growing up, a transference of wisdom and hope, so that someone else will have the kind of an opportunity I had."

In time Alwyn became the national spokesman for PRIDE Canada (Parents' Resource Institute on Drug Education), supporting programs to prevent drug and alcohol abuse. He also helped set up other organizations aimed at helping young Native people, including the Aboriginal Sports Circle and the Alwyn Morris Education and Athletic Foundation. He twice won the Tom Longboat Award for Canada's outstanding Aboriginal athlete, was appointed an ambassador

Alwyn Morris, outstanding athlete, the day he was inducted into the Sports Hall of Fame.

of youth for Canada, and named to the Order of Canada. In 2000, Alwyn and Hugh Fisher were inducted into Canada's Sports Hall of Fame.

ABOUT THE MOHAWK

Mohawks, the "People of the Flint," are one tribe of the Six Nations, also known as the Iroquois Confederacy. They call themselves the Haudenosaunee (ho-dee-noe-sho-nee), meaning "People of the Longhouse." The Haudenosaunee are the oldest living participatory democracy on earth. The United States' representative democracy drew much of its original inspiration from the Haudenosaunee.

CHAPTER 6

Naomi Lang

(KARUK)

ICE DANCER, OLYMPIAN, AND FIGURE SKATER

Skating enthusiasts are familiar with the name Naomi Lang. After all, this ice-dance champion has been impressing audiences since she was six years old. By the time she was twenty-three, Naomi had become the first Native American female athlete to participate in the Winter Olympic Games.

Naomi was born December 18, 1978, in Arcata, California, but moved to Michigan when she was eight. She is a member of the Karuk tribe by her father's heritage, and her Karuk name is Maheetahan, which means "Morning Star."

Almost from the moment she could walk, Naomi wanted to dance. By the time she was three, she had already started ballet training. Her first performance was at the ripe old age of six, as a bonbon in Tchaikovsky's *The Nutcracker.* (This Christmas performance is a great opportunity for ballet students, as there are many roles for children of all ages.) After that Naomi danced in *The Nutcracker* every year until she was fifteen. At one audition she was chosen over almost two hundred other girls.

When she was twelve, Naomi was accepted into the ballet program at the prestigious Interlochen Arts Academy

Naomi Lang

in Michigan. At the end of that school year, she had done so well that the academy presented her with an Outstanding Achievement in Ballet award and invited her back on scholarship.

But dance wasn't Naomi's only passion. When she was eight, she attended a performance of *Smurfs on Ice* and left the arena in awe. Soon she began skating lessons and won her first skating competition—the Ann Arbor Springtime Invitational in Michigan—when she was only nine.

Naomi, age 8, at a powwow in Grand Rapids, Michigan.

A year later, not long before an important skating competition, Naomi caught pneumonia. Because pneumonia settles in the lungs and makes it difficult to breathe deeply, she was extremely tired and feverish. Did Naomi bow out of the competition? Far from it. As weak as she felt, she gave it her all and won a bronze medal.

Now Naomi was at a crossroads. She could stick with ballet and accept the scholarship to the Interlochen Arts Academy, but she was also a talented skater. How could she give up one for the other? She couldn't and she didn't. Instead she combined both her loves and became an ice dancer.

It was a tough decision. Had she stayed with ballet, her expenses would have been covered, but there were no scholarships or funding for a young ice dancer at her level. Naomi's mother, Leslie, was a single parent, and skating is a very expensive sport. Ice time must be rented. Costumes have to be custom-made, stage makeup and hair have to have a professional touch, and even beginners' skates cost almost a hundred dollars a pair. Then there is the cost of travel to and from competitions as well as living expenses while competing.

But the most important item—and the most expensive—is the right coach and choreographer. Private coaches are picky about which skaters they will work with. Fortunately, Leslie and Naomi met Sue and Eve Chalom at a skating competition in Detroit, and they all quickly became good friends. Sue's daughter Eve was being trained by the famous coach Igor Shpilband. Sue was so impressed with Naomi's talent and grace on the ice that Sue recommended her to Igor, and after watching her skate, he agreed to coach her. But there was a catch: Naomi needed better skates than the ones she was wearing, and high-quality ice-dance skates cost $900 a pair. No way! But Sue and Eve Chalom came to the rescue. Eve bought new skates and gave her old ones to Naomi.

There was only one more problem to solve. As Leslie put it, "Your average hometown does not usually have an Olympic-level skating coach." And Allegan, Michigan, where she and Naomi lived, was no exception. Since Igor was based in Detroit, Leslie and Naomi moved there. Now he could coach Naomi full time at the Detroit Skating Club.

Naomi was a natural—graceful and elegant—and was soon partnered with John Lee. Naomi and John were awarded the US Figure Skating Championships novice ice-dancing title in 1995 and the silver medal in junior ice dancing in 1996.

Talented Russian-born ice dancer Peter Tchernyshev saw Naomi skate at the 1996 nationals and was impressed. When he learned that her partnership with John Lee had ended shortly after that competition, he wrote Naomi a letter to ask if she would be interested in meeting with him. Perhaps they would make good ice-dancing partners. Naomi traveled to Lake Placid, New York, where he was based, danced with Peter, and realized they were well matched.

This discovery forced Naomi to make another tough decision. If she was to become Peter's partner, she would have to move to Lake Placid to train with his coach, Natalia Dubova. She would have to leave behind her school, her friends, and her coach. And she was too young to go alone; her mother would have to move too. Together they decided it was worth the hardships. Lake Placid would be their new home.

ICE DANCING

Ice dancing combines the formal and technical aspects of figure skating competition with the beauty and artistry of dancing. Ice-dancing partners incorporate different styles of dance and ice-skating techniques into their programs. Couples may perform such dances as the tango or the Lindy combined with difficult technical moves. This sport is ideal for anyone who likes both figure skating and the art of dance.

Lake Placid was a lot different from Detroit, and Naomi knew no one there except Peter. Going to a new high school, where she was a complete stranger, was hard enough, but in Lake Placid figure skating wasn't all-important as it had been at the club in Detroit. Hockey was the primary sport, so hockey teams got all the prime ice time. Naomi had to train whenever the ice was free, sometimes as late as three in the morning, and she still had to be on time for school! Even so, Naomi stayed on the honor roll her entire year at Lake Placid High School and received an award from the principal for excellence in citizenship.

Naomi and Peter trained hard and made their competitive debut as a senior dance team during the 1996–97 season. They came in fifth at the US nationals in 1997, an amazing accomplishment for skaters who had been together for such a short time.

Despite their success, Naomi was still lonely. She missed her friends and Igor, her former coach. After almost a year in Lake Placid, Naomi returned to Detroit. Peter soon followed, and the pair began training with Igor Shpilband and Liz Coates.

Naomi and Peter have perfected many difficult and graceful moves.

All that training and hard work paid off. In 1998 the couple came in third at the 1998 US Figure Skating Championships. In 1999, in Morzine, France, they were tenth at the Lysiane Lauret Challenge, their first international competition. For five years, from 1999 to 2003, Naomi and Peter won first place in ice dancing at the US Figure Skating Championships, and they ranked as high as eighth at the world level. At the International Skating Union's Four Continents Figure Skating Championships, they placed third in 1999 and 2003, second in 2001, and first in 2000 and 2002.

Naomi passes the torch at the 2002 Olympic Winter Games in Salt Lake City.

All championship-level athletics take a toll on the body, and Naomi and Peter were forced to withdraw from the first half of the 2001–02 competitive season after Peter suffered a stress injury. But they were determined to make a comeback because they had one more dream: competing in the 2002 Winter Olympic Games. After Peter recovered, they went back to work on the ice. On February 18, 2002, in Salt Lake City, Naomi and Peter finished in eleventh place and received a standing ovation from the Olympic audience. As they took their bows, hundreds of yellow roses rained down on the ice from the fans.

Naomi Lang had competed in the Winter Olympic Games—something no Native American woman had done before. At a reception after the finals, Utah Indian tribes honored her. Tribal leaders expressed their admiration and appreciation and presented Naomi with gifts. She had brought great honor to her tribe, her family, and herself.

In 2003, after Naomi and Peter won their fifth consecutive first place US Figure Skating Championship title in ice dancing, they temporarily retired from skating. On August 26, 2004, Naomi gave birth to a daughter, Lillia Ashlee Besedin. Lillia's Karuk name is Kuusrah Imkata'xrih, which means "Bright Moon."

On September 17, 2005, Naomi and Peter came out of retirement to perform a new program at an event to raise funds for ice-dancing scholarships. At that time they embarked on a new career as professional ice skaters.

Looking back, Naomi's mother, Leslie, says she was overwhelmed at the opening ceremonies of the 2002 Olympics

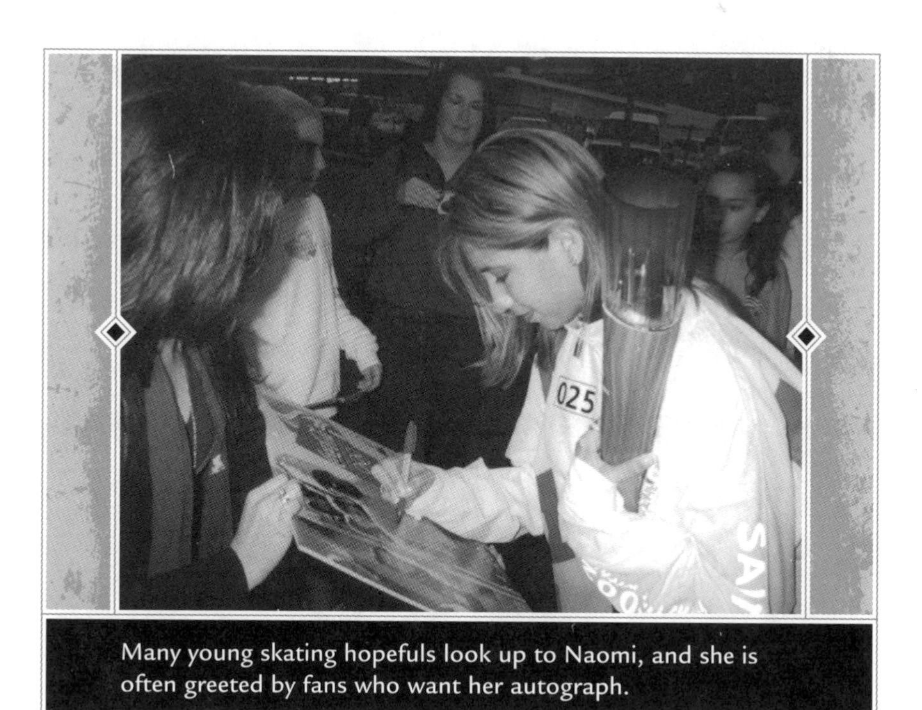

Many young skating hopefuls look up to Naomi, and she is often greeted by fans who want her autograph.

when she saw Naomi walk out as a part of the US Olympic Team. The standing ovation Naomi and Peter received after their Olympic free dance will always stand out in her mind, but there are many other accomplishments that make her proud. Looking back at her daughter's success, Leslie says, "I think of the little moments when Naomi showed good sportsmanship, congratulating and applauding a competitor who had done well. Or the many times when her coaches, fans, and friends told me what a nice person she was."

When Naomi was very young, Leslie gave her a poster of a beautiful ballet dancer for her bedroom. It states, "To be somebody special—believe that you are."

Naomi Lang is someone special. She had the determination to never give up and to prove that through persistence, passion, and hard work, anything is possible.

ABOUT THE KARUK

The Karuk persist with astounding vigor in northwestern California. The traditional center of the Karuk world is where the Salmon and Klamath Rivers come together. Karuk are important players in managing wildlife and protecting sacred sites.

CHAPTER 7

Beau Kemp

(CHOCTAW AND CHICKASAW)

PROFESSIONAL BASEBALL PITCHER

Beau Kemp is a soft-spoken young man who enjoys wearing a cowboy hat, plaid shirts, and a large belt buckle. As a kid, he posed a threat to his competitors in many sports before being scouted by the Baltimore Orioles, picked up by the Minnesota Twins, and then traded to the Toronto Blue Jays.

Sebastian "Beau" Kemp was born on October 31, 1980, in Claremore, Oklahoma. Beau's mother was a teacher at his high school. His father, who is Choctaw and Chickasaw, energized his ability in sports. "My dad went to a boarding school, and he never really had anything except sports. He was a basketball player and still plays basketball today."

Like many kids from families with no money to spare, seven-year-old Beau spent his free time at the local Boys Club. There were a lot of Native American and African-American children there, as well as at his school. Everyone mixed in pretty well, so Beau did not personally experience much racism. By the age of eight, while Beau was the pitcher and shortstop with the Boys Club team in Broken Arrow, Oklahoma, he was picked up by the Tulsa Rangers, a sponsored team. As Beau explains, "A sponsored team is more com-

Beau Kemp

petitive and travels both in and outside the state to various towns and tournaments. And the sponsors pretty much pay for everything: brand-new uniforms, even new gloves—and this is for kids eight and nine years old!"

The Tulsa Rangers went to the Little League World Series in Atlanta, Georgia, and came in fourth against some tough, powerful teams. "We had some rain, and helicopters would come and dry off the field. That was a big deal. I don't think I ever saw anything like it before or since. And seeing teams from all over—teams from Puerto Rico and California—was also a big deal."

When Beau was eleven, the Tulsa Rangers won the Dizzy Dean World Series in Chattanooga, Tennessee. "It was unbelievable. We won it pretty confidently. I pitched in that championship game."

Beau had proved himself a worthy player and was a member of a sponsored team every season until he was fourteen. Little League teams traveled a lot, so Beau got to see many places he would otherwise never have been able to visit.

Beau was the only freshman on a team of seniors. He was the number-two pitcher, second only to Brad Penny, who has played for the Los Angeles Dodgers and the Chicago White Sox. "I pitched all four years, and in my sophomore year, we won state. I ended up getting all-state player of the year in 1997."

For most of his young life, he had been an intense competitor in football and basketball, as well as baseball. In fact Beau had been so impressive, he received competing college offers to play different sports.

He wanted to make the right choice. He also wanted to be successful and make his father proud.

"I always wanted to please my Dad. He was really driving for me to be a basketball player. He knew me, and he knew what I was capable of doing, whether I was letting up or not. Sometimes he would push me and I'd get upset, but that was exactly what I needed.

"I signed a football scholarship to Northeastern Oklahoma A&M College to play quarterback. I was going to go there for two years, and then I was going to go to Oklahoma State. I was verbally committed to them to go there for football after I finished my schooling at NEO."

Beau's decision about his future got easier after he and his Amateur Athletic Union high school baseball team, the Kansas City Monarchs, won the AAU National Champion-

BASEBALL

Known as the all-American sport, baseball's name refers to the four bases that form a diamond shape around the pitcher's mound. In baseball, a batter attempts to hit a pitched ball that is thrown over home plate. Points are scored if a baseball is hit without being caught and the batter runs a complete revolution around the bases. Baseball's influence is far reaching: in literature it was popularized in the poem "Casey at Bat," written by Ernest L. Thayer, and the familiar 1908 song "Take Me Out to the Ball Game" is still sung at baseball games today.

ship, and Beau was awarded Most Valuable Player of the tournament. "That was the biggest moment of my life. I was pitching, and I got two or three hits. When the score was tied, I hit a little dribbler down third and just ran as hard as I could. I couldn't see what was going on, but I was like, man, I'm going to beat this out, and if we beat it out, we're definitely going to go up a run. And I ended up beating it out. I'm pitching and that's all I needed—to get up one run. I pretty much knew I had my A-game. So I was right there. And we won the game."

That series was the deciding factor: Beau's future would be in baseball. Meanwhile the big-league scouts were watching. "Out of high school I was drafted by the Baltimore Orioles, but I just held out. I don't know why but I did. It was just a gut feeling."

It could have been his only chance to sign with a major-league baseball team, but Beau had faith in himself. He was determined to be a success on his own merit and his own

Beau pitching for the Red Wings.

terms. "I talked to Baltimore but just didn't want to sign with them. And they were like, 'Okay. We're just going to put you back into the draft.'"

After high school Beau decided to go to Saddleback Junior College in Orange County, California. "I played for the Saddleback team in the Orange Empire Conference. It's a real competitive league. There were scouts there when we played ball, and the Twins ended up getting me in the thirty-first round. So I was like, okay, this is what I want to do. I'm going to go into professional ball. I know that's exactly what I want to do now, and I'm going to do it."

Now that's self-confidence.

Once accepted by a professional baseball team, players climb the ranks of minor-league clubs. Beau climbed quickly. "There are two rookie ball leagues. Then there's A-ball. Then there's Double-A. And then there's Triple-A, and then the big leagues. My first year I went to rookie ball, and I was there for almost a month before going to higher rookie ball. That team was the Elizabethtown Twins. We won our league, so I ended up winning another championship. The next year I went to Quad Cities.

"Every year I moved up a level, but I remember a real breakout year in High-A in the Florida State League. I had had a zero ERA that whole year. I ended up throwing a 0.6 ERA, with twenty-nine saves. That was a good year."

On his way up the ladder, Beau was named minor-league pitcher of the month, was selected to Baseball America's Class A all-star team, and finished the season as a pitcher with eight straight scoreless appearances covering eight innings. He pitched for the Twins' Triple-A Rochester Red Wings in the 2006 season and went 7–4.

In November 2006, Kemp was traded to the Toronto Blue Jays and signed to a minor-league contract.

When Beau talks to kids who want to be professional athletes, he tells them, "You have to be really, really committed. You're going to go through some adversity and some trials, but you can just have fun. If it's fun, everything will work out. There's going to be other kids playing, but you have to decide whether this is what you really want to do because it's going to be your life. It's a way of life, and you're going to have to be ready for it.

"Everybody wants to get there, but it's not easy. It takes a lot of sacrifice, and a lot of listening to older people who are helping you out. Listen to your coaches; and listen to people who have been there, who want to help you. Just make sure you listen to them and be obedient. They're just there to try and help you. Be coachable."

Beau has obviously followed his own advice. Sebastian Beau Kemp demonstrated self-confidence and discipline in his determination to make the most of his life choice. And that is what has made him such a great success.

ABOUT THE CHOCTAW AND CHICKASAW

The Choctaw people are experiencing a renaissance of traditional cultural arts, educational achievements, and progressive economic developments. The Choctaw have a vibrant economy sustained by a variety of industries and strong partnerships with many Fortune 500 companies.

The Chickasaw Nation is a democratic republic in which registered voters elect a governor, lieutenant governor, and thirteen-member tribal legislature. The jurisdictional territory of the Chickasaw Nation includes more than 7,648 square miles of south-central Oklahoma.

CHAPTER 8

Shelly Hruska

(MÉTIS)

RINGETTE TEAM CANADA

If you mention ringette in the United States, you are likely to get little more than a quizzical look or a shrug. But in Canada almost everyone has heard of the game and many have played it.

As a five-year-old, Shelly Hruska, a Métis from Winnipeg, Manitoba, had never heard of ringette either until some girls

Shelly Hruska

in her dance class suggested she try it. Being adventurous, she did, and she loved it from the start.

Ringette is a fast-paced team sport on skates. It's played on a hockey rink, and the object is to score goals. Players use a straight stick, similar to a broomstick, to pass, carry, and shoot a rubber ring instead of a puck. The highly competitive game requires the speed and skill of hockey, but there is a big difference: no body contact is allowed.

Ringette is hugely popular in Canada and a half dozen other countries. Because there is no checking (slamming or crashing into another player), it is predominantly played by girls and women, but its popularity among boys is on the rise. Invented in 1963 by the late Sam Jacks, who was director of parks and recreation in North Bay, Ontario, ringette is now played by teams in Finland, France, Russia, Sweden, and the United States. Nevertheless, it is still most popular where it began; there are tens of thousands of players and more than two thousand teams in Canada.

The most talented ringette players can advance from winning their provincial or territorial championships to competing in the nationals. The team that becomes national champion can represent its country in the world championships.

Shelly Hruska has achieved all this and more. Almost from the time she could walk, Shelley had been involved in figure skating as well as tap dancing and ballet. In her neighborhood, she would also play softball, baseball, and ringette.

One of Shelly's earliest memories is of trying out for a ringette team. She made the team in the Bunny Division for ages seven and younger, although she's not sure how. "I only knew how to skate on figure skates. I was so bad on regular skates that my parents put me into power skating."

Even though Shelly felt she was not a very talented player, she enjoyed the cooperative team environment and the closeness and camaraderie of her teammates.

"I wasn't very good at all, so I wondered why I started and then kept at it. Years later I asked my parents about that. They told me a story about what happened. 'One day one of your teammates picked up your stick and put it in the ring for you because you couldn't do it yourself. It was like a big sister coming over and helping you.'"

Shelly steadily improved, and by the time she was ten, she had become obsessed with the game and was a serious competitor. She played every year and at every level. Whenever she moved to a different part of Winnipeg she made an A-level team, even though she was a complete unknown. "I had played for a lot of years, so I was more skilled than some of the girls. A really good player can dominate, but I always passed the ring to the people who didn't have very much experience to help them improve."

Shelly's experience on school teams helped her to get to the national competitions.

Shelly slides in and scores!

By the time she was fourteen, Shelly was a confident player. That year in the playoffs, her A team came up against Alberta. "We were super young, and they were three years older than we were. We gave them their only loss all year and by more than one goal!"

At fifteen Shelley made the Assiniboine Park-Fort Garry Sixers, one of the AA teams that compete at the provincial level. The APFG Sixers won the provincial champions and became Team Manitoba at the nationals. In subsequent years, when her team did not win the provincial championship, Shelly was always asked to join the team that represented Manitoba.

As her dedication deepened, Shelly's record became even more impressive. Finally she set her sights on the Canada Winter Games, a competition in which the top athletes in the country vie for national championships in Olympic-style games and other sports. Shelly and Team Manitoba won the silver medal at the 1999 games.

By 2002 Shelly could feel the world championship competition within reach, and she tried out for Team Canada. She made the team and proudly wore the uniform emblazoned with a large Canadian maple leaf. But this was no

Learning to skate fast and well in a bulky uniform can be a challenge.

easy championship. Team Canada was up against some very tough opponents: Sweden, Finland, the United States, and E. H. United (the Edmonton host team). Team Canada had lost 5–4 to Finland in the previous world championship in 2000, and the Finns had assembled another formidable team for this competition.

The early games were tough, but Team Canada won against Sweden, Finland, E. H. United, and the United States. The championship match pitted Team Canada against Finland again. In a sold-out stadium, thousands of fans cheered on the two strong rivals. The crowd almost brought the house down when the final buzzer sounded. Team Canada had outscored the Finns three goals to one and brought home the gold medal!

Shelly was a key player when Team Canada again claimed the gold at the World Ringette Championship in Stockholm, Sweden, in 2004. In all, this young athlete has played at the national level for nine consecutive years, claiming four medals and four all-stars along the way. Shelly even has her own ringette trading card with her professional statistics and team colors.

"I know a girl at the University of New Hampshire; she's playing hockey there. She's been a ringette player all her life. She loves the game and would never pick hockey over ringette. But because the university offered her a hockey scholarship, she accepted. She does enjoy both games. But if you asked her which one is her favorite, she would always choose ringette. I think more kids would be involved in the sport if there was the potential to earn your living as a professional. Now there is the National Ringette League (NRL) in which you play against different provinces, but players do not get paid. There's not enough publicity—not a lot of other countries know ringette exists. It is very popular in Canada, but it dies at the border."

Shelly plays out of pure love for the sport. She hopes to promote ringette in other countries so one day the number of international players and their fans will be large enough to enable professionals to be paid. "It's such a great game," Shelly says spiritedly. "Once you get addicted to it, it sticks with you and you love it forever."

Shelly enjoys some noncompetitive time with fellow ringette players.

Shelly is now a certified level-two ringette coach and has been an instructor at the Lisa Brown's Ringette Retreat, which is based in Calgary, Alberta. She teaches eighth-grade math and science in Winnipeg and coaches all-girl volleyball, basketball, and soccer teams. She and her ringette-playing friends were on rival teams until they played together in the Canada Winter Games. Through ringette, these former opponents were brought together by what Shelly calls "the fastest game on ice."

ABOUT THE MÉTIS

There are over 350,000 Métis Nation citizens in Canada. The Métis share a history and a common culture of song, dance, dress, and other customs. They have a unique language called Michif that combines Cree and Canadian French, which emerged over two hundred years ago. Michif solidified as a language sometime between 1820 and 1840.

CHAPTER 9

Jordin Tootoo

(INUIT)

NATIONAL HOCKEY LEAGUE STAR

Nunavut—"our land" in the Inuktitut language—is one of three territories in the Canadian North. It is a vast land, larger than Ontario and more than five times the size of Texas, and it is covered with snow and ice eight to nine months of the year. There you can find mountains, fjords, glaciers, polar bears, Arctic wolves, caribou,

Jordin Tootoo

and seals. But Nunavut is also home to nearly thirty thousand people, and most of them will tell you that their most famous citizen is Jordin Tootoo, the first Inuit to make it to the National Hockey League.

Jordin's hometown is Rankin Inlet, a community of just over two thousand people on the shores of Hudson Bay. In the summer, the sun barely dips below the horizon; in the winter, it can be dark almost all day long. Jordin often tells children that his house is so far north, it's the first stop for Santa Claus on Christmas Eve.

When he was a kid, Jordin loved hockey, whether it was on the street or inside the rink. His father, Barney, had been a well-known player for the semipro Thompson Hawks. He handed down his knowledge of the game to Jordin and supported his son's decision to pursue hockey. "He pushed me every day to become a better player," Jordin recalls.

But school came first in the Tootoo household. If Jordin didn't make good grades, there would be no hockey. He remembers, "Schooling was huge in our family. Without an education nowadays, it's pretty hard to find a job. I wouldn't say I was an A student, but I got my work done on time, and if it wasn't good enough, my parents would drive me to do better."

Jordin's dad was a licensed plumber with the territorial government and the maintenance man for the hockey arena. For two years, beginning when he was twelve, Jordin would leave home at six each morning to shovel the snow from around all the town's government buildings before school. The job took about two hours, often in minus 40-degree weather. It wasn't the best climate to work in, he says, but the job gave him spending money.

It seems natural that Nunavut would produce outstanding hockey players, but the climate creates some unique problems. During the winter the wind chill can drop to minus 76 degrees F (minus 60 degrees C) and there's little daylight, so playing outside is not an option. Rankin Inlet does have a covered hockey arena, but when Jordin was growing up, it didn't have a refrigeration system. The ice surface didn't freeze until November, and by April it would be melting.

The location and size of Rankin Inlet adds to the difficulty. Because it can only be reached by boat or plane, playing in a league against teams from other towns is not practical. And because it's a small town, there is only one team for each age group, so the kids end up playing scrimmage.

Jordin always looked forward to the highlight of the hockey season: "Once a year we would fly to another community or a community would come to our town, and we would have a weekend tournament for kids who were eight to twelve years old. Our community always dominated and won the championships."

In order to play real games during the rest of the season, the younger kids would play against the older ones. Barney knew how to play a rough game and told his son that if

ICE HOCKEY

Ice hockey is a fast and intense game played on an ice-covered rink. Players wear padding, helmets, and skates, and they score points by propelling a rubber puck into a well-guarded net with the use of a hockey stick. Talented athletes possess the ability to make quick turns and quick stops and pass the puck with agility to other players. It is an extremely popular sport in Canada and the United States.

he wanted to play against the older kids, he would have to be able to hold his own. Jordin learned fast, applying his father's lessons to his advantage.

In 1997, when Jordin was fourteen, he left home to play in the more competitive AAA Bantam League in Spruce Grove, a town of almost nineteen thousand people just outside Edmonton, Alberta. He had never been in such a large place. Everything was new, including racism. Groups of kids would yell at Jordin and his friend Justin Pesony that Natives were not going to take over their school. Jordin took out his frustrations on the ice.

For the first time Jordin was playing with kids his own age. His coaches kept telling him to tone it down, that he was too rough, and that he had to stick to the rules. But Jor-

Jordin speeds across the ice toward the goal, with his opponent following in close pursuit.

din didn't know the rules. (Back home the kids made them up as they went along.) Jordin may have lacked knowledge, but he made up for it in spirit, and his passion paid off. The next season, when he was fifteen, he joined the junior A league. Jordin was the youngest player on the team, yet at the end of the year he was voted the most popular player by the fans.

After two seasons, at the age of sixteen, Jordin was selected forty-third overall by the Brandon Wheat Kings in the Western Hockey League Bantam Draft. "I just got a phone call one day," Jordin recalls, "and they invited me to camp. The first two years I was there we weren't the greatest team, but then we made it to the semifinals twice." During his time with the Brandon Wheat Kings, Jordin was described as "one of the most menacing players in the WHL" and led the team in penalty minutes with 216. Yet he was also a high scorer, was voted Most Popular Player four years in a row, and was loved by the Wheat Kings' fans—if not by the competition.

Jordin had a solid 2002–03 season, posting 74 points in fifty-one games. In 2003 he was named a WHL Eastern Conference first team all-star. He played for Team Canada in the 2003 International Ice Hockey Federation World Junior Championships and was a key player in the team's silver-medal win. He was also honored with the special youth award at the 2002 National Aboriginal Achievement Awards.

When he was eighteen, something amazing happened: Jordin was drafted into the National Hockey League. The Nashville Predators chose him in the 2001 fourth round. (The Predators are based in Tennessee—a far cry from the ice and snow of Rankin Inlet!) Jordin played for the Predators' farm team for two years before finally making the roster after his third Predators' training camp in 2003. But even before he stepped on the ice in his first game, against the Anaheim Mighty Ducks, sportswriters and fans were

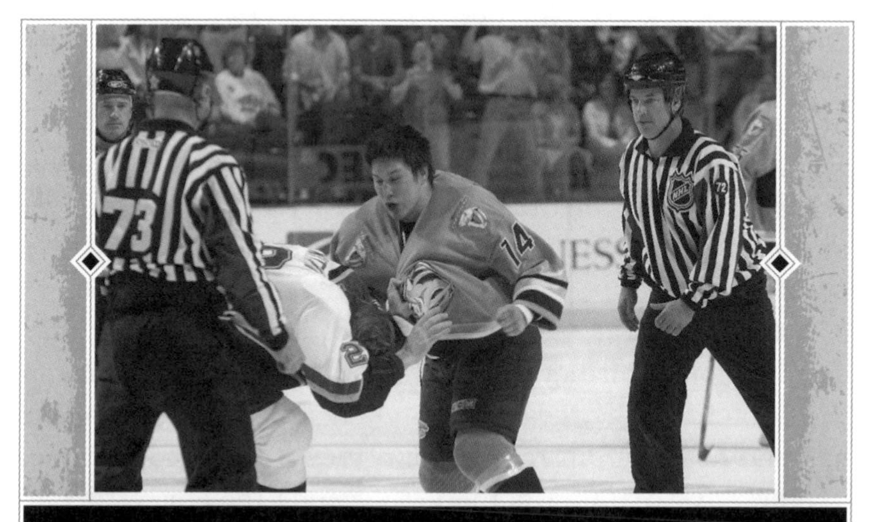

Jordin's rugged, hard-hitting play does not take away from the fact that he is a talented player.

concerned about his size. At five feet nine (1.75 m), Jordin is small for a hockey player, but he has been described as a "human torpedo." As he puts it, "I play with a big heart, and that's all that matters."

At that first game in October 2003, two busloads of friends and family from home showed up to watch. His mother and father were there, cheering the loudest.

Jordin's rugged, hard-hitting style did not take away from the fact that he was a talented player. A few games into the season, when he scored his first NHL goal, against Atlanta goalie Pasi Nurminen, Jordin was elated. "It was definitely a relief." Jordin gained a reputation as a player who could disrupt the rhythm of the other team as well as hold his own against much larger players. His scrappy playing helped the Predators make it to the playoffs.

He spent eight seasons with the Predators. In 2012 he signed with the Detroit Red Wings and in 2014 with the New Jersey Devils.

Jordin credits hard work and determination with getting him where he is today. In 2011 he established the Team Tootoo Fund to help a variety of charitable causes that support at-risk youth. He often speaks to groups of young people, encouraging them to hold on to their dreams. He has been the spokesperson for the National Aboriginal Role Model Program, which reaches out to younger kids and teenagers to help them achieve. "You've got to pick the right people to hang out with. My true friends are the people who help me pursue my goal." He also believes teenagers need to realize that even though they think parents are always on their backs, those parents really want to help. They are mentors. "If it wasn't for the backing of my mom and dad, I wouldn't be here today. They've supported me in every decision I've made."

Jordin Tootoo's Inuit name, Kudluk, means "Thunder." Watching him thunder down the ice, chasing his dreams, it seems that name couldn't be more fitting.

ABOUT THE INUIT

For five thousand years, the Inuit people have occupied a vast territory stretching from the shores of the Chukchi Peninsula of Russia eastward across Alaska and Canada to the southeastern coast of Greenland. They have thrived by their ability to utilize the physical environment and living resources of the Arctic. The relationship between the people and the land continues to define Inuit culture and identity.

CHAPTER 10

Ross Anderson

(CHEYENNE-ARAPAHO, MESCALERO APACHE)

FASTEST SKIER IN NORTH AMERICA

Ross Anderson, who bills himself as "the Fastest American Indian on Mother Earth," is also the fastest speed skier in North America. Anderson was born May 8, 1972, on Holloman Air Force Base near Alamog-

Ross skis in the Champion De Monde at Les Arcs, France, 2001.

ordo, New Mexico. His parents, who were Cheyenne-Arapaho and Mescalaro Apache, were very young at the time and realized it would be best for Ross if they gave him up for adoption to people who would be better able to take care of him. A Caucasian family in Colorado adopted Ross and raised him in the skiing hub of Durango, Colorado. At the age of three, Ross began lessons at an alpine skiing school there, where he learned slalom, giant slalom, downhill, and speed skiing. He began racing competitively when he was just six.

It's not as though Ross faced much discrimination, but Durango is a typical resort town frequented by wealthy, predominantly white tourists. "Not many Natives live in Durango, and I definitely felt out of place because I was the only dark person on the ski team, the only dark person at the resort. If I saw someone else who was dark, it was a miracle. It was like, 'Hey, let's take a picture!'"

The closest place for Ross to learn about Native culture was from the Southern Utes nearby. Although they were helpful, Ross still felt as if he didn't quite fit in. "You look around. You see magazines. You see commercials. You don't see Natives whatsoever, and you always wonder, 'Why am I different?' You almost get depressed because your skin is not like everyone else's you grew up with. That's why I became who I am. I was going to do what I was going to do in a sport that had no people of color—period."

Ross's adoptive father had been a ski racer in college and later joined the ski patrol. Ross was not far behind; he raced in slalom, giant slalom, and downhill events. But he was drawn to something more dramatic. Initially it was ski jumping. Ski jumpers charge down a long ramp at extremely high speeds, lift off, and jump as far as possible. "You see a nice ramp and then there's nothing there. And then the next thing you see is the bottom of the hill. You ask yourself, 'What am I doing here?'"

Ross Anderson

Ross was obsessed with skiing. When he was a teenager, if he couldn't get to the ski lift, he would hike up a mountain near his home and ski down, maneuvering around oak trees as if they were gates. (This is not recommended! One wrong move could mean serious injury or death.) He would compound the risk by skiing until it was too dark to see.

Although skiing was his passion, Ross enjoyed other activities as well. After finishing high school, Ross became a member of Up with People, a multicultural singing and dancing troupe, for a year. The group consisted of four hundred people representing thirty-two countries. Ross got to travel all over the world, dancing and acting in skits and interacting with various cultures. The itch to travel has never left him.

He started college, but after a year he felt he had to choose between becoming a professional skier and finishing his schooling. Ross chose skiing—his taste for speed was too great to give up the sport. At twenty-one years old he became a professional. A friend who had competed in the 1992 Olympics told Ross that speed-skiing time trials were being held in Donner, California. Ross had read about downhill speed skiing in magazines but had never tried it.

Downhill speed skiing is the world's fastest nonmotorized sport: at speeds exceeding 150 mph (241 kph), a run on a one-mile (1.6-km) course can take less than fifteen seconds. Skiers are required to wear a specially designed helmet, boots, oversized skis, and a skintight, customized suit that takes forty-five minutes to put on. The ski poles are custom bent around the body and filled with lead so they don't fly off or break under the pressure from speed and wind.

Ross had none of this necessary equipment. He bought a motorcycle helmet and a used suit and drove nonstop to Donner, California, getting there just in time to register. "That's where it all started. I qualified at about 78 miles an hour (125 kph), and that was it. Speed skiing is cool. It's different, it's extreme, and I felt I could get good at it. That's why I stuck with it. Besides, there's little presence of anyone of color, and it's at the World Cup level."

It didn't take long for Ross to become a force to contend with, and he was soon participating in international competitions. Overseas many competitors had to look twice;

Ross in his specially designed suit and gear.

they had never seen a Native American on the slopes. They were curious and respectful, unlike a few of Ross's American teammates. Some US rivals tried to discourage him, saying such things as "You're not going to be the fastest" or "You're never going to be good enough, so you might as well go home." Such comments just gave Ross extra impetus to succeed.

With experience he better understood the sport and gained speed. "A lot of it is technology, a lot is experience and knowing exactly what to do—how to work with the wind, Mother Nature, the suit, your tuck. Everything is a factor—the wax under your skis, your poles, what type of day it is, what the temperature is. Everything."

A 1998 race turned into a speed skier's nightmare for Ross. At 131 mph (210 kph) he hit the finish line . . . and then an indentation in the snow. The wind lifted his left ski into the air like a wing. Wind caught the side of his heel and whipped him around on the ground. Suddenly he was spinning so fast that his suit melted, his flesh burned, and his skis splintered. A doctor patched him up, and Ross raced the next day. He doesn't remember how he placed in the race—that didn't matter. The important thing was that he put skis on and competed.

In 2001 Ross headed out for ten weeks of speed-skiing competitions in France and Italy and became the first Native American to stand on a world-championship podium. In the 2001 European professional speed-skiing tour, he became the number-two downhill speed skier in the world!

For the next few years, Ross continued to compete ferociously and pulled off a bronze medal at the 2005 International Ski Federation World Cup. In 2006, in Switzerland, he broke the United States record, reaching 154.06 mph (247.9 kph).

Ross says that it was his ability to focus that helped him break the record. "When I was up at that start on the final run, I was so focused that I actually had difficulty hearing the crowd roar. The sound certainly travels, but I was so focused I could barely hear it."

SPEED SKIING

An extreme sport, to say the least, speed skiing first began in 1931 with the Kilomètre Lancé speed events in Switzerland. Leo Gasperi won the competition with a downhill speed of 84.723 mph (136.348 kph), enough to get a serious speeding ticket on almost any highway. Today speed skiers suit up with special equipment, such as aerodynamically designed helmets; boots; specially made elongated skis; lead-filled poles; and skintight, polyurethane-coated, polypropylene ski suits. Competitors can now reach speeds of over 150 mph (241 kph), not a speed in which anyone would want to wipe out!

Ross described a run at incredible speed like this: "Everything has to be just right at the beginning. You get in your tuck, and you make sure everything is sealed—your helmet, your armpits on your knees, the whole bit. You look up, just a glimpse to see that you're on line. Then you put your head down, bury it, and go until you see a red line. Ten feet in front of you is all you're going to see. When I see that red line, I know I'm about finished and stand up. You have to trust yourself and everything around you—that's one of the things I love about the sport. You can get good at it, but you can't be the best at it. Nobody can because every day is different."

Ross recently found out who his biological parents are. His birth father died some years ago; his birth mother lives in Michigan. He has discovered that he has a very large family and intends to learn more about them and his ances-

Ross (right) wins the bronze medal at the World Championships in Cervinia, Italy.

tors. He also wants the family to get to know his daughter, Sierra Star. "My adoptive parents were supportive of me getting in contact with my birth family, so that made it a lot easier."

Ross has focused on giving back to the Native community. At the Durango Mountain Resort, he hosted a Ski with Ross Anderson Weekend to give Native youth an opportunity to ski. He has been the ambassador for the Native Voices Foundation, which provides slope access and skiing and snowboarding equipment. He has been featured on television and in magazines and appeared in the 1998–99 Warren Miller documentary film *Freeriders*.

A role model to Native youth, Ross wants the Native youth of today to realize that they too can succeed. "Sticking with it is one of the main things I've known to do all my life. And I hope kids who read this will realize that if they stick with their subject or their dreams or whatever they want to do in their lives, there will definitely be accomplishments. Follow your dreams!"

CHAPTER 11

Stephanie Murata

(OSAGE)

CHAMPIONSHIP WRESTLER

Stephanie Murata is a wrestling champion—and we're not talking the showbiz wrestling of the World Wrestling Entertainment (WWE), with choreographed fighting, outlandish costumes, and insults shouted over giant loudspeakers. Stephanie is a hard-nosed, in-your-

Stephanie Murata

face, serious freestyle wrestler with honed technique. She's also been the United States National Women's Wrestling Champion eight times!

Stephanie Murata was born May 16, 1970, in San Mateo, California, into a large Osage family: her parents, James and Connie; brothers Patrick and Scott; and sisters Ali and Alex.

She has faced a lot of discrimination but not the kind you might have expected. "Most of the stuff related to being a Native American has been fairly positive; however, my sport is a male-dominated one, and there are a lot of people who would like it to remain that way."

Stephanie has always been athletic. Initially she played soccer with one or more of her brothers. "My first real team was called the Mighty Maroons—not the Mighty Morons, the Mighty Maroons. Nearly every girl on our team ended up going on to play college sports." Stephanie liked playing striker and halfback, both positions that involve a lot of running.

At Mercy High School, Stephanie swam, ran track, and played soccer and volleyball. Mercy, an all-girls Catholic school in Burlingame, California, was in a fairly small league, and Stephanie went to regional and conference competitions in nearly every sport she played. "In track I did the 100-meter hurdles only because, when my coach was teaching us hurdles, she told me, 'You're too short. You can't do it.' So of course that was what I wanted to do."

Stephanie sought advice from coaches of rival schools at track meets. The coach from Presentation High School made a big difference. "She was coaching a girl against me, and this girl was getting better. So I asked this coach, 'How are you supposed to train for this?' She told me and I got better. The stuff that she did worked." That's hardly a surprise: later on that same coach became the coach of the 1996 Olympic track and field team.

FREESTYLE WRESTLING

Wrestling's roots reach back to 3000 BC, having been found illustrated on ancient pieces of art. Wrestling competitions are or have been a part of the Olympics, the world games, the National Collegiate Athletic Association, and the Amateur Athletic Union. In freestyle wrestling, participants try to hold or pin down their opponents to gain points or win the match. Competitors are not permitted to grab clothing in order to secure a hold during the match.

After graduating from high school, Stephanie entered the University of California, Davis, originally to major in animal science. "I wound up with a degree in genetics, but I still finished the certification in animal science and received a minor in nutrition." Her extra studies meant a fifth year at college. She had played college soccer and was a member of the ski team, but after four years she was no longer eligible for university athletics. It was then that Stephanie's roommate made her an interesting offer.

The girl was a wrestler and the daughter of a European wrestling champion. She knew that Stephanie was an avid athlete and said, "I'm going to Phoenix for a tournament. Why don't you train for it and we can go together? I'll ask my sponsor to pay for your ticket. It could be fun." Stephanie recalls, "I said 'OK, I'm doing this for you. I'll train. I'll learn what I'm supposed to do, but I'm not going to spend any money on it.' I was a typical college student. I had no money. She said that was fine."

Stephanie had agreed to wrestle before she had even tried it, and she had just two weeks before her first tournament to learn as much as she could. She was strong and fast. "I had no expectations, which was just as well because my opponent took me down very fast. I had no idea what a bridge was so I ended up getting pinned. The next day I was more sore than I have been in my entire life. Everything hurt."

Nonetheless, she did well enough to be listed as an alternate for a European tour. When one of the wrestlers was unable to go, Stephanie found herself on the US Women's Wrestling team.

Stephanie considered herself lucky to have entered wrestling when she did. Only a few years earlier, women wrestlers had to pay their own way to competitions. "There was one girl whose father had taken a second mortgage out on his house so she could compete and train and do everything that all the girls are getting funded for now. It was a male-dominated sport, and it still is."

Having qualified for the European tour, she was invited to a training camp for a wrestling club named the Sunkist Kids, based in Arizona. "The coach at Arizona State was not for women's wrestling at all, but he slowly came around. He ended up helping me train and coaching me on technique."

Stephanie wrestles Clarissa Chan in the finals of the 2006 Senior Nationals.

Stephanie had three weeks to train for the nationals. "I came in third or fourth, but I got to train with the six-time world champion from Japan."

After the nationals, Stephanie was asked to wrestle for Sunkist Kids, and she received help from a sponsor. By 1996 she had improved immensely, yet in her final match of that year's national competition, she had a hard time focusing. "I remember thinking, 'Oh, so-and-so must have gotten a haircut,' instead of thinking about the match. The girl I was wrestling did a collar tie that was really hard and that kind of snapped me out of it, brought me right into the moment."

With her attention back on the competition, she won the match and took the title. After that the awards poured in. Stephanie was a two-time Pan American Games champion and the United States National Women's Wrestling champion seven years in a row—1996 to 2002! (She won again in 2005.) In 2001 she won the silver medal at the World Wrestling Championship in Bulgaria.

Stephanie Murata

By 2004 Stephanie Murata had been the national champion seven times, had been on nine world teams, and was a candidate for the 2004 Olympics. She now found herself under the direction of coach Sergei Beloglazov, a six-time world champion wrestler and two-time Olympic champion for Russia. But at first Sergei would have nothing to do with her. "He said he was not a woman's coach; he was the men's coach. I could come to the men's practices sometimes, but that was it.

Finally, two years later, he said, 'OK, OK, you can call me your coach.'"

Women's wrestling had been proposed for inclusion in the 2000 Olympics, but the International Olympic Committee opted for weight lifting instead. In 2004 the committee opened up four wrestling spots for the women.

While Stephanie was in the Ukraine that January for the Golden Grand Prix, she got a staphylococcus bacterial infection in her knee and required emergency surgery to save her leg, so the rest of her season suffered. This could have been a major disappointment, but she was happy just to have her leg!

Stephanie was hopeful that, with Sergei's coaching, she would win a spot on the 2008 Olympic team, but Sergei decided to go back to Russia—ironically to coach women's wrestling. "It was very difficult for me because one of my goals was to go to the Olympics, but I was really excited for him. I knew their program was going to do wonderfully. They were really fortunate to have him, especially because he had said he would never coach women."

When not competing, she traveled to camps and clinics on freestyle wrestling for girls, and in 2013 she was on the medical team at the USA Wrestling Junior and Cadet National Championships in Fargo, North Dakota. As a physician's assistant in Hawaii, Stephanie now works with athletes on the national and state wrestling teams.

The eight-time national women's wrestling champion remains an inspiration to young female athletes. "You have to believe in your dreams, and you have to try to achieve them," she tells them. "If only one person gets to go out of a hundred thousand or even five million—you could be that one person. You could be the one who makes it. If you don't try, you're definitely not going to be that person."

Stephanie Murata is that person and more.

THE OSAGE

A traditional Osage Nation buffalo-skin shield appears on the state flag of Oklahoma. The shield has seven eagle feathers suspended against a sky blue field.

CHAPTER 12

Jim Thorpe

(SAUK AND FOX)

AN AMERICAN LEGEND

Jim Thorpe is one of the greatest athletes of all time. He excelled in track and field, wrestling, baseball, and football, and was an avid horseback rider. His talent and determination took him to the 1912 Olympics and professional baseball and football careers.

Jim's father, Hiram, was Sauk and Fox; his mother was Potawatomi with blood ties to the Kickapoo. Jim was born in the spring of 1887 on reservation land in Oklahoma, and he was named Wa-Tho-Huk, which means "Bright Path."

That same year, the US government passed the Dawes General Allotment Act in an effort to end the Native concept of holding land communally and considering it a gift from nature. The act declared that land had to be owned by one person. Reservation land was chopped up and given to individuals to do with what they pleased. As a result, much Native land was lost because many of the new owners sold their land to non-Natives. When Jim was two, the family moved to their allotment, where they raised horses and cultivated corn, pumpkin, and other vegetables as food for the family and feed for the animals.

Jim Thorpe kicking football, October 28, 1912, at the Carlisle Indian School vs. Toronto game.

In 1893 Jim and his two brothers had to attend a boarding school near Stroud, Oklahoma. Like other schools of its kind, the Stroud school's main purpose was to assimilate Native students into the European-American culture. Discipline was strict and Native languages were forbidden. Jim hated the harsh, regimented life. In his third year he ran away and went home, but his father disciplined him and sent him back to school. The only solace was that Jim's older brother, George, and Jim's twin, Charlie, were also at Stroud.

In the winter of 1896, Charlie contracted pneumonia and smallpox. He died in the spring, and Jim was overcome with grief. He had lost not only his twin brother but also his closest friend. Jim ran away from school again.

This time his father sent him hundreds of miles away to the Haskell Institute, a military-style government school in Kansas for assimilating Natives into the larger society. Students were up at 5:45 a.m. every day. They were taught basic writing, math, reading, history, and science, but much of the day was devoted to learning a practical skill, such as baking, blacksmithing, cooking, farming, or wagon building. Native languages were banned, as were rough play and joking around. Jim was miserable, but there was one thing about Haskell that he did like: sports, especially baseball and football.

In the summer of 1901, Jim's father was shot in a hunting accident, and Jim wanted to see him. He ran away from school and hopped a train that was going the wrong way! It took him two weeks to get back to Oklahoma. By the time Jim got home, Hiram had recovered enough to be furious with him.

Jim ran—with nowhere to go.

He was fourteen years old and alone, with absolutely nothing. He found work in Texas tending horses and eventually was able to buy his own team. Jim took the team back home and reconciled with his father. Shortly after he arrived, however, his mother died, and Jim stayed on to help his father run the farm.

In 1904, at age seventeen, Jim decided to go to the Carlisle Indian Industrial School in Pennsylvania; however, his stay there started out badly. His father died, and Jim was too far away to get home for the funeral. He left Carlisle for a few years and went home to run the farm. But at Carlisle he had met Glenn "Pop" Warner, a man who would change his life. Warner is a football legend who did much to transform the game, but he was most interested in building athletes' characters, no matter what their sport.

The 1911 Carlisle Indian School Football Team. The football reads "1911, Indians 18, Harvard 15." Jim is in the second row, third from the right.

Jim returned to Carlisle where he found that perhaps all that running had done him some good. During the school's annual track and field competition, Jim came in first in the 120-yard hurdles and second in the 220-yard dash. But his sports career really blossomed when he happened to see the school track team practicing the high jump. None of them could clear the bar at five feet nine inches (1.75 m), but Jim asked if he could try. He cleared it easily (work clothes and all) and found himself on the Carlisle track team!

From that point on, his life changed. Jim was no longer required to work in the school summer labor program; instead he was free to train. Jim enjoyed the Carlisle track team, and in the last meet of the following season, he earned his varsity letter, breaking all previous Carlisle records.

When Jim tried out for football practice that fall, Pop Warner was concerned that this small-framed track star might not do well against larger players. But when he was given the ball at the tryouts, Jim was easily able to dodge would-be tacklers down the entire length of the field. Then, just for good measure, he turned around and did it again . . . in the opposite direction.

Warner realized he had a great running back, and Jim quickly became a star player. He immediately discovered an amazing benefit of being on the varsity squad: he moved into the athletic dormitory, an elite setup with pool tables, study rooms, and huge amounts of great food. Jim was in heaven—and his grades were rising, too.

Jim and some of his friends played minor-league baseball during the summer months. The wages were only about fifteen dollars a week, but Jim had such a great time that he considered not returning to Carlisle. Two things drew him back: Pop Warner would allow him back on the football team, and he would coach Jim for the upcoming 1912 Olympic Games in Stockholm, Sweden. At school track meets, Jim was unstoppable, winning eleven gold, four silver, and three bronze medals in the 100-yard dash; 45-, 120-, and 220-meter hurdles; the standing, broad, and high jumps; and the 12- and 16-pound shot puts.

At twenty-five years old, Jim qualified for the Olympics, participating in the pentathlon, which consisted of 200- and 1500-meter races, the long jump, the javelin throw, and the discus throw. Jim won the long jump, placed third in the javelin, and threw the discus a full three feet (1 m) farther than his nearest rival. He won the 200-meter and the 1500-meter races. Jim so far outperformed his competitors that he would be taking home a gold medal!

The following week brought the decathlon, which involved ten events over three days. The first day was rainy and the arena was slippery. Jim came in third in the 100-meter

Jim in his track uniform, posing as if on the mark in a track event.

dash and second in the broad jump, but he led the shot put by two feet (.6 m). Jim finished the day with a slight lead. The next day Jim came in first in the high jump and fourth in the 400-meter race. Then he set a record with his first-place finish in the 110-meter hurdles and held on to his lead.

Some of the third-day events were not Jim's strongest, but he still managed to come in second in the discus and third in both the javelin throw and the pole vault. The final event was the 1,500-meter race. Jim was exhausted from

The 1912 Homecoming Victory Parade in honor of Jim Thorpe and Louis Tewanima, a Hopi who won the Olympic silver medal for distance running. "Pop" Warner rides with them. An Indian drill team marches behind.

three days of competing, but he ran it in an incredible 4 minutes and 40.1 seconds to win—and beat his own previous best time.

When the decathlon points were tallied, Jim had an amazing 8,412.96 points out of a possible 10,000—almost 700 points more than the second-place finisher. When he stood on the podium (twice) to receive his gold medals for the pentathlon and the decathlon, there were huge ovations from the crowd. King Gustav V of Sweden, who presented the gold medals, said, "Sir, you are the greatest athlete in the world."

Jim responded with a simple, straightforward, "Thanks, King."

When Jim returned to the United States, he was a hero, honored with a ticker tape parade on Broadway. Jim recalled, "I heard people yelling my name, and I couldn't realize how one fellow could have so many friends." But in 1913, a newspaper published a story about Jim having been paid to play baseball. The Amateur Athletic Union decided that Jim had competed in the Olympics illegally. His gold medals were taken back and his statistics removed from the Olympic record books.

Jim was crestfallen. He signed with the New York Giants, but baseball was not to be his only game. Two years later he also was playing professional football. His baseball career included three seasons with the Giants, a stint with the Cincinnati Reds, and another spell with the Giants before his last season of Major League Baseball with the Boston Braves in 1919. Meanwhile, he helped the Canton Bulldogs football team win a professional championship in 1916, and in 1919, he kicked a 95-yard winning field goal for Canton that many claim was the greatest kick ever made. He joined the Cleveland Indians baseball team in 1921 and the Chicago Cardinals football team in 1929.

In 1920 Jim was elected president of the American Professional Football Association (later the NFL). A year later he organized the Oorang Indians, an all-Native professional team. Six years later, at age forty-one, he retired from professional sports but appeared as a guest of honor at the 1932 Olympics and was treated to a standing ovation.

In 1950 the Associated Press voted Jim Thorpe the greatest athlete of the first half of the twentieth century, and the following year, Burt Lancaster starred in a movie about Jim's life, *Jim Thorpe—All-American*. Sadly, Jim Thorpe suffered a heart attack and died on March 28, 1953.

When his family wanted to bury him in Oklahoma and build a memorial to him, state officials refused. Jim's widow, Patricia, had heard about a small Pennsylvania town called Mauch Chunk that wanted to change its name to one that would draw tourists. She contacted the officials there and

Jim played baseball with the New York Giants, the Cincinnati Reds, and the Boston Braves. This photo is from around 1915.

took her husband's remains to be buried in the renamed town of Jim Thorpe, Pennsylvania. His monument there bears the King of Sweden's famous remark, and the town holds a birthday celebration for Jim each May. After his death, the National Football League named a most valuable player award in his honor. He was named to both the professional and college football halls of fame.

In 1982, seventy years after Jim's Olympic victories and nearly thirty years after his death, the International Olympic Committee restored Jim Thorpe's gold medals to his family and his Olympic records to the record books. Jim Thorpe finally received the honor due to "the greatest athlete in the world."

ABOUT THE SAUK, FOX, AND POTAWATOMI

The Sauk, Fox, and Potawatomi all speak Algonquian languages. The Potawatomi originally lived as hunter/gatherers because they were too far north for reliable agriculture. Fighting over trade during the Beaver Wars in the mid-seventeenth century drove the Potawatomi south into what is now Wisconsin. There Potawatomi women learned how to grow corn, beans, and squash from the Sauk and the Fox. The Potawatomi added medicinal herbs to the crops under cultivation.

CHAPTER 13

Delby Powless

(MOHAWK)

PROFESSIONAL LACROSSE PLAYER

Imagine being told you were too short to play the sport you love. Would you give up? Imagine being told you are too short and too slow. Are you ready to quit? Now imagine you were told you were too short, too slow, and too skinny. That's what everyone told Delby Powless, yet he became a champion and the first player chosen in the 2005 National Lacrosse League entry draft.

No one really knows when lacrosse was invented. It was already being played by the indigenous people of North America at the time of the first European contact. Two groups of players would try to injure their opponents with a hard, quickly thrown ball hurled from a scooped-out stick. The contests were an important part of spiritual and physical life, a means of settling disputes and training for war. One Ojibwa myth even tells us that the game was responsible for winter (and therefore, migration)

Delby playing on the Rutgers University lacrosse team.

because Loon lost a lacrosse match to Hawk, and all the birds on Loon's team were forced to fly south, away from the cold that Hawk brought to the land.

Since winter does come, whether by Hawk's doing or otherwise, lacrosse was quickly adapted as an indoor game. Called "box lacrosse," it is played in hockey arenas—without the ice—by five players and a goaltender in three twenty-minute periods. It is a fast, team-oriented sport, a marriage of lacrosse and hockey.

"Canadians love lacrosse," Delby explains. "It's got the rough-and-tumble aspects of hockey. My favorite part is the competitiveness of it and scoring goals. I'm only five foot six and 177 pounds (1.67 m and 80 kg), so I'm not the guy who is going to run people over. And I'm not going to be running by people. Setting people up to score is the way I contribute to my team."

Delby is a Mohawk. He was born in 1980 and grew up on the Six Nations of the Grand River Territory near Brantford, Ontario. Like many of the Mohawk kids his age, Delby seemed to have been born with a lacrosse stick in his hand, but he initially set his sights on playing in the National Hockey League. Even though he played in organized lacrosse at the age of five, Delby says, "Lacrosse was more of a fun sport. My friends and I would play all summer, three or four hours a day. We didn't look at it as practice—it was our way of having fun. We didn't even realize that it was going to make us better players."

When the Six Nations Minor Lacrosse team played against non-Native squads, racial slurs were fairly common. "At times you would hear the odd 'wahoo' or 'wagon burner' from kids who didn't know any better. But it would really get upsetting when you would hear parents say things like 'Go back to the reserve.' Parents are supposed to know better."

Size and speed are usually a great advantage in lacrosse, but Delby and his young friends were soon more than the non-Native teams could handle. By the time Delby was sixteen, his team had won the Ontario Midget A championship two years in a row, losing only two games out of sixty. Many games were won by twenty goals because of the players' well-practiced skills. In fact the team was so good that it was studied by coaches from other leagues.

"One parent coached a peewee team in Mississauga, which is forty-five minutes away. He brought his entire team to every tournament to watch us play. The coach would point things out, especially about our goalie. He was my cousin and the best goalie in the province at the time. We were only four or five years older than these peewee kids, but they were absolutely impressed with us. And they knew all our names. That was cool because they were a non-Native team."

When Delby's midget team won the Ontario championship the second year, the Six Nations Arrows Junior A team finished in tenth place. (Junior A is the highest level for players seventeen to twenty-one years old and the league from which players are drafted by professional teams.) But

LACROSSE

It has been called the fastest game on two legs. Introduced by the Iroquois, lacrosse is now hugely popular in Canada and the United States. In 1994 lacrosse was declared Canada's official summer sport. Players use a netted stick to shoot balls into a tended goal. The ball travels at incredibly high speeds, which is evident by the heavily padded goalies. You have to stay alert to watch this fast-paced sport!

when Delby and many of his teammates moved up to the Arrows the next year, the team rose to third in the league.

After high school graduation and three years in the juniors, Delby decided to go to college. He was too late to apply to Division I colleges in the United States, so he opted for a community college, Herkimer County Community College, in upstate New York. There he met coach Paul Wehrum.

"He was one of the biggest inspirations of my career. Playing for him was a life-changing experience. When I left to go to college, I wasn't headed in the right direction. I was partying a little too much. I wasn't doing well. I had to get away from the reserve."

Delby needed to change his life, and Coach Wehrum was the person to help him do it. The coach asked him what kind of person he wanted to become, and he said if Delby took care of things in the classroom, Wehrum would take care of things on the field.

"It was easy. All I had to do was listen to what he said. I put in the work for the first time. Lacrosse had always come naturally to me, so I'd never been a hardworking player. The same thing with school. I was a bright kid—people said so—but I never put in the work to get good grades. In high school I had a C average. When I went to college, I realized that if I wanted to go to a good Division I school, I was going to have to get good grades. Plus I was going to have to do well in lacrosse and stay out of trouble."

At the end of his first year, Delby was named a First Team All-American. He had a B-plus average, led his team in goals, and was key in getting his team to the Division III regional championships. The following year, Delby was named team captain and, as the team's leading scorer, was again named a First Team All-American.

At the end of his second year in Division III, Delby had his sights set on Maryland's Towson University, but he was

Delby Powless

recruited by Jim Stagnitta, the new coach at Rutgers University. He was willing to give the small Canadian a shot.

Delby's first game for the Rutgers team, which was ranked thirty-second, was against, ironically, Towson, which was ranked tenth. The game was in February in miserable, near-blizzard conditions. Delby scored three goals, leaving the teams tied 9–9 at the end of regulation time. In sudden-death overtime, Delby scored on his first possession.

"Everybody was going crazy. The parents were flipping out. After I got off the field, the first thing I did was call Coach Wehrum. I had to tell him he was the first person I thought of when I scored. He could not have been happier. It was probably the best feeling I had ever had."

Delby's leadership led to Rutgers' ranking jumping to ninth in the country, the school's highest ranking since 1990.

In 2003 the young athlete was featured in *Sports Illustrated*'s "Faces in the Crowd" section and also won a silver medal in the World Indoor Lacrosse Championship, playing with the Iroquois Nationals in Toronto. "We were playing for our people, and people were really proud of us." The same year he was presented with the Tom Longboat Award, given to the best Aboriginal athlete in Canada. It had previously been awarded to two other Powless lacrosse players—his great-uncle, Gaylord, and his cousin Ross.

After the 2004 Rutgers season, when Delby received an honorable mention as a lacrosse All-American, he transferred to Brock University in St. Catharines, Ontario, planning to become a teacher. His team won the Canadian University Field Lacrosse Association Championship, and Delby was named All-Canadian. "As far as I know, I'm the first person to have been named All-Canadian and All-American!"

Delby was the 2005 first-round draft choice for the Buffalo Bandits of the National Lacrosse League. He played for the Bandits in the winter and for the Six Nations Chiefs of the Ontario Lacrosse Association in the summer. Delby helped the Bandits win the NLL championship in 2008. In 2009 he joined the Toronto Nationals.

Delby now runs Powless Lacrosse, a specialty sports store, and continues to be an inspiration to young athletes. In 2005 he coached his old high school lacrosse team to their first Class B championship. "I probably felt more proud of the guys on that team than when I played myself." He has also reached out to youth through his work with the Dreamcatcher Charitable Foundation.

His message to youth is simple, direct, and true: "Don't let anybody ever tell you that you can't do something. Whenever someone said that I was too small or too slow, I would just use it as motivation. But if I had not done well in school, I would never, ever have been where I am today. All it took was one coach. He sat me down and set me straight."

THE MOHAWK AND LACROSSE

The original Mohawk name for lacrosse was *tewaaraton*. The National Collegiate Athletic Association (NCAA) chose this name for the Tewaaraton Award, which is presented to the top college lacrosse player. The bronze trophy features a Mohawk man in traditional dress. The Mohawk Nation Council of Elders has endorsed the Tewaaraton Award.

ABOUT THE AUTHOR

In addition to serving as the executive vice president and co-owner of Schilling Media, Inc., a Native American media-relations corporation, Vincent Schilling is an enrolled member of the St. Regis Mohawk Tribe; an award-winning Native American author, producer, and photojournalist; and a public speaker who has traveled throughout the United States and Canada.

Vincent is the host of "Native Trailblazers," an online radio program for indigenous people that airs Fridays at seven p.m. (EST) on blogtalkradio.com/NativeTrailblazers. He has contributed hundreds of articles to national publications and websites, including Indian Country Today Media Network, *Native Peoples* magazine, and *Winds of Change*. In 2011 Vincent won a bronze EXCEL Award for the *Winds of Change* article "Conflict on the Mountain." He was also presented a human rights award by the mayor of Virginia Beach, Will Sessoms Jr., for programs about Native American issues in the Hampton Roads region.

Vincent Schilling

Vincent has shared his knowledge and wisdom with public, governmental, and private entities, talking about diversity in schools and the workplace and overcoming the stereotypes of Native American people today. His work has introduced him to a multitude of fascinating people, from athletes to entertainers.

Vincent lives his wife, Delores, in Virginia Beach. You can follow him on Twitter at twitter.com/VinceSchilling.

Aboriginal Sports & Wellness Council of Ontario

ASWCO.ca

ASWCO promotes healthy living and offers training, certifications, and support for coaches, athletes, and other organizations in each of Ontario's six regions.

Native American Recreation & Sport Institute (NARSI)

charismapros.com/p/narsi.htm

NARSI offers the best youth recreation and sport directors and coaches training programs in America. The emphasis is on training adults to work with children ages five to fourteen, with a focus on the emotional, physical, spiritual, and cultural development of these children.

NDNSPORTS.com

The goal of this site is to promote awareness about Native American athletes competing in a wide variety of college and professional sports to the public and Native community online.